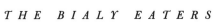

THE BIALY EATERS

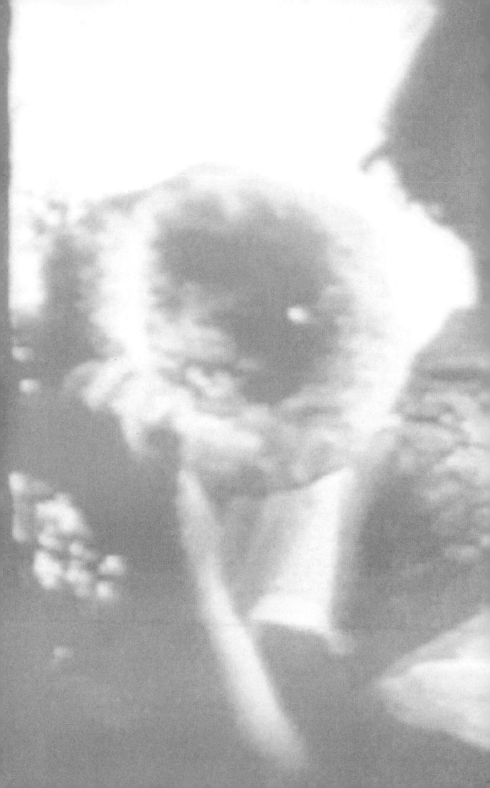

THE
BIALY EATERS

━━━━⟫•⟪━━━━

*The story of a bread
and a lost world*

━━━━⟫•⟪━━━━

MIMI SHERATON

BROADWAY BOOKS
NEW YORK

BROADWAY

Broadway Books titles may be purchased for business or promotional use or for special sales. For information, please write to: Special Markets Department, Random House, Inc., 1540 Broadway, New York, NY 10036.

BROADWAY BOOKS and its logo, a letter B bisected on the diagonal, are trademarks of Broadway Books, a division of Random House, Inc.

Visit our website at *www.broadwaybooks.com*

Grateful acknowledgment is made for permission to reprint:

Young girl with Bialystoker kuchen from film, *Jewish Life in Bialystok*, 1939. Courtesy of The National Center for Jewish Film at Brandeis University.

Library of Congress Cataloging-in-Publication Data
Sheraton, Mimi.
    The bialy eaters: the story of a bread and a lost world / by Mimi Sheraton.
        p. cm.
    Includes index.
    1. Bread. 2. Cookery (Bread) I. Title.
    TX769 .S413 2000
    641.8'15—dc21   00-034276

FIRST EDITION
Designed by Songhee Kim

ISBN 0-7679-0502-4
00 01 02 03 04 10 9 8 7 6 5 4 3 2 1

Portions of this work have previously appeared, in a somewhat different format, in *The Bialystoker Shtimme* and the English edition of the *Forward*.

For all of

the Bialystoker kuchen fressers

and their vanished way of life

ACKNOWLEDGMENTS

This book would have been impossible to do without the
generous help of dozens of people all over the world who
shared their memories of bialys and Bialystok with me.

The most encouragement and information in the earliest
stages of my research came from the late Izaak Rybal, who
was the director of the Bialystok Center and Home for the
Aged in New York and who published the account of my
search in his semiannual magazine, *The Bialystoker
Shtimme,* which led to so many valuable contacts. Invaluable
assistance was provided by Danny Scheinin of Kossar's
Bialys (a.k.a. Kossar's Bialystoker Kuchen Bakery) in New
York. I am also indebted to the late Dr. Anatol Leszczynski
of Warsaw and Tomasz Wisniewski, the historian, journalist

and archivist in Bialystok, Poland, both of whom provided valuable leads.

Some of the most eloquent remembrances came from Samuel Pisar of New York and Paris, the late Max Ratner of Cleveland, and from Roy M. Mersky of Austin, Texas.

Leo Melamed of Chicago showed extraordinary patience as I badgered him for ever more details of his memories of Bialystok, as did Ben Halpern of Detroit, my oldest respondent who was 101 when I last interviewed him, shortly before his death in September 1999. I am grateful to his daughter, Barbara Levin, for keeping us in touch. The Yiddishist David I. Gold was most helpful on the semantics of the bialy.

Friends and respondents in Israel who helped immeasurably include Sussi and Herbert Pundik, Dalia Lamdani, who is the astute food journalist writing for the magazine *Laisha*, Avinadov Lipa and his bialy-pita baker Mordecai Zananni, Arie Shamir, Yerachmiel Giladi and Giora Raz, a chef, caterer, and photographer.

In Paris, I appreciated the interview with Charles Zabuski and later received added insights from his niece, June Sutz Brott in California, who coauthored her uncle's autobiography.

Friendly and generous Australians who helped were the late Paul "Pesach" Szmusz, whose memory was awesome, Ursula and Felix Flicker, and the writer, Arnold Zable.

In Buenos Aires, Anita M. Weinstein, a director of AMIA (Associación Mutual Israelita Argentina), searched for and found helpful respondents such as Velvl Matinsky and his wife, Mina Yabkov, Armando Bublik, and Abrasha Levy. At the Yivo Institute for Jewish Research in New York, I will always be indebted to the late Dina Abramowicz, the former librarian, and her successor, Aviva Astrinsky, to whom I was introduced by Max Gitter, a New York attorney who has done considerable work for Yivo, of which he is a board member.

Both Krysia Fisher, the photo archivist at Yivo, and Yale J. Reisner of the Ronald S. Lauder Foundation at the Jewish Historical Institute in Warsaw, Poland, tried to help unearth photographs of bialy bakers and their shops in Bialystok before the Holocaust. My biggest disappointment is that none could be found, even though I contacted many museums and cultural institutions around the world.

I am grateful to Miko Sloper of the Esperanto League in Emeryville, California, for his advice on the correct spellings and forms in that universal language. The Jewish historian Barbara Kirshenblatt-Gimblett led me to some Yiddish linguists early on. Michael London of Mrs. London's Bakery and Cafe in Saratoga Springs, New York, generously gave me tips for perfecting a home recipe for bialys.

Judah Engelmayer and Danny Cohen, the new owners of Kossar's, tirelessly answered many questions about changes being made in the bakery and details of how bialys are baked. Rabbi Daniel Alder of the Brotherhood Synagogue in New York kindly informed me on matters of *kashrut*. Gina Piers, my Polish-born dressmaker, worked diligently to put me in touch with the most helpful Roman Powlowski, an editor at the Bialystok newspaper *Kurier Poranny*.

James Ratner, the son of Max Ratner, carefully filled me in on family details after his father's death. Dalia Carmel, an Israeli living in New York, was kind enough to use her Hebrew to check facts with Israeli respondents.

Rabbi Leonard Blank of the Bialystok Center did his best to verify some statistics. Judge Martin Shulman, the president of the Bialystoker Synagogue in New York, spent an evening giving me a tour of the *shul* and recounting its history.

Ilene Rosenzweig, now a style editor at the *New York Times,* gave this story its start by publishing the account of my visit to Bialystok when she was the feature editor at the *Forward.*

I doubt that this book would have come into being without the patient, careful shepherding of my wonderful agent, Dan Green. The vision of Harriet Bell, formerly my editor at Broadway Books, did much to shape this book. Gerald Howard added important insights when he took over the work-in-progress.

ACKNOWLEDGMENTS

Most of all, perhaps, now as always, I must thank my husband, Richard Falcone, for bearing with me throughout this long and sometimes seemingly irrational project, and for accompanying me and keeping me sane on so many of these far-flung searches.

CONTENTS

⟶⟩●⟨⟵

⟶⟩●⟨⟵

INTRODUCTION

"When I was an adolescent in Auschwitz lying on the hard shelf that was my bed and hallucinating from hunger, I would often try to recall the shape and savory aroma of the kuchen we used to eat at home in Bialystok. By then I had lost all of my family and school-friends. Years later, when I was in New York, I would often watch those street-corner wagons that sell coffee and bread in the morning. I marveled at the whites, blacks, Asians, and Latinos as they munched on their bialys. I felt as though I was from another planet. To each of them, it was simply a tasty snack. How could they know they were partaking of something sacred—a bread that evoked bittersweet memories of a cultured and tragic corner of eastern Poland? A bread that, in my psyche, summons up even today the mystical dream world of Marc Chagall and Isaac Bashevis Singer."

—SAMUEL PISAR

On a gray and rainy day in November, 1992, I stood on Rynek Kosciuszko, the deserted town square of Bialystok, Poland, and was suddenly overcome by the same shadowy sense of loss that I had felt in the old Jewish quarters of Kazimierz in Cracow and Mikulov in Moravia. To anyone who knows their tragic history, these empty streets appear ominously haunting, especially in the somber twilight of a wet, gray afternoon. The damp air seems charged with echoes of silent voices and ghostly wings and the minor-key melodies of fiddlers on rooftops.

As a slight chill went through me, I had vague intimations that I was at the beginning of an adventure. I could not guess, however, that what had started as a whimsical search would lead me along a more serious path that I was unable to forsake for seven years. Even now I am not sure my quest is over, nor that I want it to be.

The story began with my passion for the squashy, crusty, onion-topped bread roll known as a bialy and eaten as an alternative to the bagel. Widely popular in New York City and, to a lesser extent, elsewhere in the United States, the small, round bialy is characterized by an indented center well that is ringed by a softer, higher rim, all generously flecked with toasted onions and, at its most authentic, with a showering of poppy seeds. I cannot remember when I first ate one of these fragrant rolls, but surely it was addiction at first bite, starting with the mouthwatering scent of onions and yeast and the crisp bread's affinity for sweet butter and fluffy cream cheese.

Knowing that the bialy's full and official name was Bialystoker kuchen and that it originated in Bialystok, a city in northeastern Poland that belonged to Russia until 1918, I wanted to make a pilgrimage to that town and sample the roll on its native ground. A fortuitous assignment to report on Polish food for the *Condé Nast Traveler* magazine made such a side trip a reality in 1992.

My desire to learn what a bialy might look and taste like in its place of origin was one of many such quests I have made during the past forty years. What some might consider gastronomic obsessions are partly a sort of hobby, prompted by simple curiosity. But, inevitably, there are professional concerns, for as a food critic, I look for the best and most authentic products and preparations to serve as benchmarks. As exhausting as such doggedness can be, I value these culinary treks because they lead to people and places I might not otherwise have encountered.

My interest in authenticity began in Copenhagen in 1953, when I suddenly realized that the flaky yeast puff pastries served with breakfast coffee at the Hotel D'Angleterre were the originals of what we in the United States mean by Danish pastry, never mind that the Danes called that buttery miracle wienerbrød, Vienna bread. Soon I went on to France, where I couldn't resist ordering pain perdu to see how the French made French toast, and, later to Istanbul, where I sampled the colorful, gummy candy we call Turkish delight and was stunned to find that the native product actually tasted of the fruits that colored it instead of just plain sugar. (My interest, to be clear, is in prepared foods, not in simple ingredients, such as Scotch salmon or Parma ham.)

As an adjunct pursuit, I also look for varying interpretations of ethnic classics as they emigrate from native grounds. It was in Paris, also in 1953, that I first saw gefilte fish elegantly done as a whole, stuffed, aspic-glazed fish instead of as the round dumplings we know, the French spin being a revelation. And I have found that even a so-called New York bagel is vastly different in Los Angeles, to say nothing of Italian pizza as rendered in Paris, Munich, Hong Kong, and Dallas.

The result of my initial quest for the bialy in Bialystok is described in detail in the pages that follow. My reports on that search appeared in several publications and brought forth dozens of letters from Bialystoker émigrés around the world. Some had left their homeland in the early part of the twentieth century, understandably disheartened by years of prejudice and pogroms, but most were Holocaust survivors. All were eager to share memories of the kuchen that was the literal and figurative staff of their lives, the icon that recalled home, family, and childhood friends and evoked an unrequited yearning for a lost world. Many also said proudly that throughout Poland and neighboring Lithuania and what is now Belarus (formerly Byelorussia or White Russia), they, the Jews of Bialystok, were nicknamed *Bialystoker kuchen fressers*, prodigious eaters (*fressers*) of those oniony bread buns.

So, although I first wanted to seek out the original bialy in Bialystok, later, as I learned of the far-flung *landsleit* (countrymen) in Melbourne, Buenos Aires, Tel Aviv, and Paris, I wondered how bialys would differ in such disparate outposts.

It is not surprising that memories of a simple and runty onion roll should have evoked the bygone world of Bialystok Jews. To make a rather obvious comparison, the bialy worked in my research much as the madeleine did for Proust, although I feel that the pallid, effete recollections of a hermetic world summoned up by that spongy, sweet, shell-shaped cake do not hold a candle to the feisty and earthy experiences recalled by this yeasty, crusty roll. Most of the inhabitants of Proust's lost times were as fragile and delicate as the madeleine. The Bialystokers I encountered comprise a tough, resilient, streetwise bunch, cynical for the best of reasons yet full of broad humor, the very qualities one might expect of those whose palates are strong enough to tolerate a tough, charred roll topped with browned onions first thing in the morning.

Few aspects of life inspire such persistent nostalgia as the foods of one's childhood, reminders of the joyful security of home and family. The phenomenon is acknowledged by the Chinese poet-statesman, Lin Yutang, who wrote, "What is patriotism but the longing for the foods of one's homeland?" Many times when interviewing total strangers, I have found that if I could get them to talk about the foods they grew up with, they relaxed, dropped their guard, and became trusting, and they developed instantaneous feelings of friendship because the subject seemed so benign.

Among such foods, none has greater resonance than bread. It is so fundamental for survival in the Western, bread-eating world that it is accorded spiritual significance in many religions. In his classic work, *Six Thousand Years of Bread, Its Holy and Unholy History*, H. E. Jacob writes, "The Jews made bread the starting point of their religious and social laws." As punishment for the Fall, the cast-out sinners henceforth would know "the bread of affliction," and much of the Jewish Passover observance revolves around unleavened bread. A weekly ritual in religious Jewish homes is the *motzi* prayer, said with the cutting of a new loaf of the braided challah at dinner on Friday as the Sabbath begins. The most obvious example of bread's spiritual importance in the New Testament is the Eucharist, commemorating Jesus' admonition to his disciples, "Eat! I am the bread of life." And among both Jews and Christians of Eastern Europe, there persists the superstitious custom of taking a gift of bread and salt to a new home—bread for basic sustenance, salt for variety and spice. (In my family, it was also customary to take a candle, promising light and warmth.)

For several different assignments, I have gathered ethnic breads in New York City, and on each foray I collected about seventy-five varieties in the five boroughs alone, varying in size, shapes, toppings, and dough content and representing European, Latin, and Middle Eastern countries. All were very much alike in nutritional value, but bread is not bread alone. Apparently all émigrés long for the bread of their homelands, to nourish the psyche as well as the body.

I was reminded most dramatically of bread's role as a true soul food in 1994, when I stood in front of the dizzying display at Abulafia, the bakery established in 1890 in Old Jaffa, near Tel Aviv. Each day, shelves and baskets overflow with Middle Eastern breads, including Yemenite pita spread with the spice mix za'atar, and some glazed with cheese or topped with fried eggs, and the feta-stuffed turnovers, sambusaks. There are ka'ahks (large sesame-encrusted rings also known as bagelech in Israel), and ridged oval sheets of Iranian bread strewn with pungent black onion seeds, and big blistered rounds of Iraqi pita that look like free-form ceramic bowls. And in the Carmel Market in Tel Aviv and the Mahane Yehuda market in Jerusalem, bakeries also offer challahs, the long or round rolls known as bulkas, mountainous, dark pumpernickels, and heavy corned or sour ryes, and more, all for the Ashkenazim of Eastern Europe. Israel is made up of immigrants from about ninety-two countries, and it appears that the bread from each is available to make strangers feel at home. It could be said that the rivalry for political power between the Sephardim and the Ashkenazim in Israel is expressed by a bread rivalry. Perhaps the growing supremacy of the Sephardic pita over the raised Ashkenazic loaves is a portent of things to come.

Small wonder, then, that the flavor, scent, and feel of the oniony bialystoker kuchen, so much a staple in the Jewish diet in Bialystok, should recall a lost world. That it took me over seven years to discover that world was due to the far-flung outposts of the Bialystokers I sought, and because I was dependent on various writing assignments to finance my journeys, always allowing extra time to pursue what really interested me most. The research has been thoroughly intriguing and seemingly endless, with almost every interview leading to further fascinating clues. How could it be otherwise when the subject is as yeasty as bread and life?

As my research stretched out through the years, I began to feel as if my own roots lay in Bialystok, although clearly they do not. Three of my grandparents came from other parts of Poland, and a fourth from Germany. Perhaps, having eaten so many bialys, I finally became a Bialystoker by ingestion, and, in contrast to the lotus eaters of Homer's Odyssey, who grew content, indolent, and forgetful after indulging in that fruit, a bialy eater becomes inextricably linked with a sadly distinguished and unforgettable past that now feels like my own.

As I read and listened to recollections of that past, I could not stop. Each story and each memory struck me as being different, incredible, and worth preserving. Explaining how he ate kuchen as a child in Bialystok, Samuel Pisar, a most eloquent respondent who is a renowned international lawyer, said, "When we spread butter or cheese on the kuchen, it was very important that we did not lose even one tiny poppy seed. Absolutely every single one counted."

As does every single story of every Bialystoker kuchen fresser who generously shared memories, both sad and joyful.

Whitey Aquanno shaping bialys at Kossar's Bialystoker Kuchen Bakery, New York, 2000. *Photograph by Yasushi Egami.*

O N E

———————>●<———————

T H E   S T A R T E R

What would a bialy taste like in Bialystok? That is what I wondered as I prepared to visit Poland on a writing assignment for the *Condé Nast Traveler* in October, 1992. To find out, I planned a side trip to that city and so did some advance research. My obvious starting point was Kossar's Bialy Bakery on Grand Street, the main stem of New York's Lower East Side. I knew Kossar's as the source of the very best bialys in the city and, as it would turn out, in the entire country. I called Danny Scheinin, who in 1956 took over proprietorship of the bakery from his father-in-law, Morris Kossar, a partner in the business originally known as Mirsky & Kossar. Danny immediately assured me that I would find no bialys in Bialystok, a sad fact he had learned from several friends who had visited that city and found only five Jews living there. Nevertheless, experience as a reporter had taught me the value of "eyes on," looking for oneself. I was certain that I could find at least some examples or memories of these defining rolls on their native ground. I decided to take some bialys with me so that I could show them instead of trying to describe them, in the hope that I would jog a few memories.

The cold, rainy day that I went to Kossar's to buy the bialys for the trip was a portent of weather to come throughout my visit to Poland. Danny told me of the nearby Bialystoker Center and Home for the Aged and suggested that I speak to someone there and perhaps get a contact in Poland. Because of limited time, I decided to risk an impromptu visit, and so, juggling an umbrella and a bag of twelve bialys, I walked from Kossar's on Grand Street to the Center on East Broadway and Clinton Street, rehearsing my strange request. Because it is on a rather deserted street, the Center's building, completed in 1930 when the home was established, could easily escape notice, despite the landmarked exterior's rather handsome, simple Moorish art-deco facade. An offshoot of Bikur Cholim, a philanthropic organization begun in Bialystok in 1826, the Center was a nursing home and residence for aging Bialystok émigrés. It is still functioning, with only two aged Bialystokers among the ninety-five residents, and it remains ground zero as the clearing house of information for Bialystok *landsleit* around the world. The semiannual magazine, the *Bialystoker Shtimme* (The Voice of Bialystok) is produced here with both Yiddish and English texts and goes to Bialystokers all over the world, many of whom are contributors as well as subscribers. Publication of the *Shtimme* was temporarily halted from 1998 to 2000, as funds of the Center diminished. However, intermittent publication and a revised form is under way for a readership that still numbers five thousand, albeit not all are Bialystokers.

When I explained my mission to the receptionist, she contemplated me for several seconds, as though she doubted my sanity, but then politely went in search of someone who had the time to talk to me. I got lucky. Fortunately, the person who had time was the now deceased Izaak Rybal, a tall, courtly, white-haired émigré from Bialystok who was the executive director, as well as the heart and soul of the Center. When I explained that I was a food journalist going to Bialystok to look for bialys, this gracious man looked perplexed as he asked, "Why go so far? Kossar's is only two blocks away. Delicious kuchen!"

"Better than Bialystok's?" I asked.

"Well, no," he replied with a note of longing in his voice.

"Those were bigger, crisper in the middle, and had lots of *mohn* [poppy seeds] and brown onions."

Sitting in the rather bare, dimly lighted lobby of the Center, I told him about my work and why I wanted to make the journey, even if the prospects of success looked slim. He then generously gave me the name of an old, dear friend, Dr. Anatol Leszczynski, a Jewish historian living in Warsaw, although born and raised in Bialystok.

The Great Synagogue, Bialystok, 1922. Photographer unknown. *Photograph courtesy of the collection of Tomasz Wisniewski.*

Mr. Rybal told me something of Bialystok, a city that before the Second World War was known for its good schools, with an especially respected Jewish gymnasium (high school), begun in 1920 and attended by the former Israeli prime minister, Yitzhak Shamir, who grew up in a nearby town, and for its many hospitals and social service centers that earned it the encomium "The city with the golden heart." The city had a majority population of energetic, inventive Jews involved in the businesses of textiles, leather, printing, and lumber, as well as in theater, medicine, and publishing. To succeed, many of them spoke not only Yiddish, Polish, and Russian but also German.

Mr. Rybal named a few of Bialystok's more notable Jews: Maxim Litvinov, born Meier Wallach in 1876, who was Stalin's foreign minister and then ambassador to the United States; Dr. Ludwik L. Zamenhof, an opthalmologist born in 1859 and the inventor of the international language Esperanto; Dr. Albert B. Sabin, born in 1906, who in the United States developed the oral polio vaccine named for him; and Max Weber, the painter born in 1881 who emigrated to the United States when he was ten years old. All of this was a surprising and impressive start for me because my limited knowledge of that Polish city began with bialys and ended with the character of Max Bialystok as portrayed by Zero Mostel in Mel Brooks' film classic *The Producers.*

Mr. Rybal briefly described two events I was to hear of many times. The first was the epic burning of Bialystok's Great Synagogue, built in 1908 and noteworthy for its size and grandeur, while two thousand Jews were inside. (I have since read estimates ranging from eight hundred to three thousand victims.) He called it a "celebration" by the Nazis of their entry into the city. The date—June 27, 1941—is still marked each year by memorial services in Israel and also by Bialystokers who return to that city on major anniversaries.

The second event was the courageous but ill-fated three-day uprising of the city's ghetto that had officially been established by the Nazis in 1941. Between August 1 and 3, the sixty thousand Jews in Bialystok were ordered from their homes and herded behind barbed wire, an event marked by the jeering and pillaging of many Polish neighbors. In February, 1943, after being terrorized by intermittent mass killings and tortures and the removals of thousands to labor camps, and inspired by news of the brave uprising in the Warsaw ghetto just a month before, two hundred of the ghetto's underground formed a resistance unit that operated for months. Their actions culminated in a revolt that began on August 16, and when they were defeated, the forty thousand remaining Jews were shipped to Auschwitz and Maidanek and any remaining were shot. The ghetto cemetery on Zabia Street in Bialystok was destroyed by Polish punks in 1971. Twenty-two years later, in 1993, an obelisk on the cemetery grounds was dedicated to those ghetto martyrs.

Izaak Rybal also mentioned the nearby Bialystoker Synagogue in New York, just off Grand Street on what was formerly Willett Street and renamed Bialystoker Place in 1978. The synagogue's original congregation was comprised of

Bialystok émigrés, but it now attracts Orthodox Jews of all backgrounds, including many young families moving back to this historically Jewish urban enclave for the conveniences of lower rents, kosher food stores, and restaurants and a functioning *mikvah*, or ritual bath. The synagogue is housed in a handsome rough-cut gray stone building, a landmark built in 1826 as a Methodist church and purchased by the Bialystok congregation in 1905. I was fortunate enough to be given a tour of the interior by the synagogue's president, Judge Martin Shulman, and was surprised to find it unexpectedly brilliant, with lavishly painted Italianate trompe l'oeil marbling, biblical landscapes and scenes from Jerusalem. Most unusual in an Orthodox setting were zodiac signs around the ceiling frieze. I was amused to see that a lobster replaced the crab as the symbol of Cancer, an unnoticed error that is perhaps understandable in a group forbidden by laws of kashrut (Orthodox Jewish dietary restrictions) to eat any shellfish and, therefore, unable to distinguish between different types.

My only other contact in Poland besides Dr. Leszczynski was Roman Powlowski, an editor on the local newspaper *Kurier Poranny* (Morning Courier), whose name I was given by Gina Piers, my Polish-born dressmaker in New York who got his name from a relative in Warsaw.

As soon as I arrived home with my bialys, I prepared them for the voyage. Following Danny Scheinin's advice, I knew I had to keep them dry and prevent mold by packing them in paper, not plastic. That way they would not rot, even though they would be stale and inedible after a day. I carefully dried them in a low oven for about thirty minutes, then set them on a rack on the kitchen counter so that moisture would evaporate. Just before leaving, I wrapped them loosely in paper towels and slid them into a brown paper bag that I stored in my suitcase, worried that the onions would work like a perverse sachet. During the ten days of traveling before arriving in Bialystok, I unwrapped the bialys and aired them on the dressers of hotel rooms each night, probably puzzling the cleaning staff.

The only person not puzzled by this activity was my husband, Richard Falcone, who had joined me in gastronomic quests whenever he could leave his own business as an importer of silver and china. A food lover with a taste for adventure (otherwise our marriage probably would not have lasted for 45 years), he was most enthusiastic about forays into Italy, where his parents were born. As a child of the Bronx, he, like so many New York gentiles, was as familiar with the bialy and the bagel as he was with pizza and calzone. Diagnosing my latest syndrome as Compulsive Obsessive Bialy Disorder (COBD), Dick was as keen as I was for yet another culinary search.

T W O

———⊰⊛⊱———

A D A Y I N B I A L Y S T O K

By the time Dick and I arrived in Warsaw, my bialys were about ten days old, having survived Moravia and Prague in Czechoslovakia and Cracow in Poland. Once again, I aired them in Warsaw, a city that took me by surprise first because of the prosperous, nervous bustle that swirled around everywhere, and next, because of the smartly dressed women who looked so contemporarily American. As soon as I had a firm plan for fulfilling my official assignment (meaning reservations at all of the restaurants I wanted to try), I called Dr. Anatol Leszczynski and told him I had been referred by Izaak Rybal.

He immediately agreed to meet for lunch, asking if he

———⊰⊛⊱———

could bring his wife, Janina. "I like people from New York," he said. "And besides, it gives me a chance to speak English." The impeccably dapper, gentle man and the sweetly shy woman, both in their early seventies, were delights as we shared a meal at the cozy Lers restaurant where we had thick, hot Polish mushroom-and-barley soup and the savory pierogi—pastry turnovers filled with meat and buckwheat groats or kasha. A native of Bialystok as was his wife, Dr. Leszczynski explained that he saved himself from the Germans by crossing the border and joining the Soviet army. It was a common solution that made Bialystok a busy escape route for many Polish Jews, with two hundred thousand jamming the city early in 1941 as a German victory seemed imminent.

A historian still proud of his native city, Dr. Leszczynski told us briefly of its past, including the facts that it was founded in 1320 by Prince Gedimin of Lithuania and that Jews had begun to settle in the region in the late fifteenth century, establishing a settlement in Bialystok in 1558. He also spoke of the ruling Count Jan Branicki, whose heirs ruled the Bialystok province from the seventeenth to the nineteenth centuries and gave Jews full citizenship in 1745, building a tower market of eighty-eight shops for them. He also financed the first wooden Great Synagogue, constructed in 1763.

I unwrapped two of my bialy specimens as I explained

Map of Poland. *Drawn by Jackie Aher.*

my mission and saw a slow light of recognition spread across Janina's and Anatol's faces as they recalled them from childhood. But both husband and wife noted that the kuchen had been much larger. "And with lots of *mohn*," Janina insisted. Neither knew of any being made anywhere in Poland but asked if they could have my two as mementoes, however inedible. Most helpfully, Dr. Leszczynski arranged for Janusz Mroczek, a chauffeur and interpreter, to drive us the 75 miles to Bialystok and spend the day guiding us. Without him, we could never have navigated this adventure.

Finally the day of departure arrived and our alarm rang at five thirty on a dull, gray morning as a mixture of rain and snow fell against the strange yellow glow of Warsaw's pollution-smeared sky. Between quick gulps of hot coffee, I packed two more bialys along with a letter to the Bialystok journalist, Roman Powlowski. Wrapped in raincoats, Dick and I huddled in the back of Janusz's Mercedes for the three-hour drive to that remote corner of Poland.

We rode through what seemed like an endless flat countryside, bland and drab on that sleet-drenched day. Here and there were sagging carved wood cottages that must have been antique craft treasures and, every so often, a small, bustling town with a supermarket and brightly dressed children waiting for school buses. The terrain became more interesting as we neared the outskirts of Bialystok with shadowy gray-brown forests streaked with silvery white birches, suggesting a ghostly stage set. The only signs of human life were a few intrepid wild mushroom hunters at the roadsides, selling their finds of the season's boroviks, which are among the world's most esteemed cèpes. Janusz explained that this area of Poland was known as the Podlasie, meaning "under the trees," and he described Bialowieza, a larger forest outside of Bialystok that is still home to elk, bison, and the famous "buffalo grass" that flavors the highly prized Zybrowka vodka.

We arrived in Bialystok at about nine in the morning and went to the town center, a rather dreary collection of three- and four-story commercial buildings of the sort we called taxpayers, living quarters over stores, that lined Flatbush Avenue in Brooklyn, not far from where I grew up.

At the Hotel Cristal, a popular meeting place, Janusz telephoned the newspaper for an appointment with the editor. He was not yet in, and anxious about wasting time, I decided to play show-and-tell with my bialys and took them to the middle-aged hotel desk clerk, asking if she had ever seen bread like that. After contemplating the bialys for a few minutes, she searched through a phone book and indicated a baker whom she thought made similar rolls. Although she got no answer when she called, I was certain that success was imminent, and so we drove to the bakery. Turning off the main streets, we entered what looked like a country backwater, with a few crudely built brick houses and ramshackle wood cabins, and, everywhere, half-paved roads and streets thick with oozing mud.

When my account of this trip appeared in the English edition of the weekly Jewish newspaper, the *Forward*, I received a note from Saul Bellow, saying that his parents always talked about the mud in the old country. He said that he had never really understood why it should have been described in such extraordinary terms until he went to Poznan and Cracow in 1959. "The mud was like a thick old gray soup, cold of course, and pouring into your shoes when you crossed the street. For the first time in my life I understood why East European Jews drank tea with lemon. They needed it for warmth, and a slice of lemon was most important not only for its flavor, but also because it resembled the sun they never saw. Lemon played a figurative role here, something like a reminder of the absent cosmic radiance."

We found the bakery in a grimy white warehouse but it had no retail shop and was already closed for the day. Spotting a small caretaker's house, Janusz knocked on the door. Three knocks later, a grumpy, half-asleep, half-besotted man appeared, rumpling his hair, hiking up unbelted pants, and grunting. Shivering in the sleet, Janusz explained our mission as I tried to take notes with a ballpoint pen that skidded across wet paper. Our host grumbled that all baking was done between six and eight in the morning. Finally, he produced a ledger and in it found the baker's home address but no telephone number, and he told us of a grocery store where he thought the baker's breads were sold. We tried in vain to find that shop driving half an hour through more unpaved roads and puddles.

By this time, we all thought the editor at the newspaper would be in and so went to his office. Roman Powlowski appeared, a tall, slim, and friendly man in his early thirties, wearing a tweed sports jacket and a haircut that could easily have marked him as an American preppy, although his English accent indicated that he had perfected the language in London. He read the letter of introduction from my dressmaker's nephew, and when he heard that we planned only one day in Bialystok, he said most generously, "Then we must start right away. I will go with you."

Before leaving, he introduced us to Tomasz "Tomy" Wisniewski, a stocky, dark-haired, and feisty historian, photographer, and journalist then in his late thirties, who was an authority on Jewish genealogy, landmarks, and history in the Bialystok region of Poland. I was therefore very pleased when Tomasz agreed to meet us for lunch, and I regretted not having known about him before this meeting.

Although it seemed rudely intrusive, we all decided to try our luck at the baker's home. The address turned out to be a modern but worn high-rise housing project, built of depressing gray cinder blocks so typical of Soviet institutional architecture. There was a special grimness about the graffiti on the wall: "*Juden raus!*"—or "Jews out!" Apparently to some Poles, the remaining five Jews were still five too many. No one was able to explain why the German *Juden raus* was used instead of the Polish, *Zydzi wychodzić*, or even the Yiddish, *Yidden arois!* I also felt a shiver go through me that had less to do with the cold, damp weather than it did with the steady climate of anti-Semitism that still exists in Poland. Perhaps that should not be surprising in the country that had the only pogroms occurring *after* the Holocaust, most infamously in 1945, when six Auschwitz survivors, on a train from Bialystok to Warsaw, were shot dead by what was described to me as Polish "hooligans," and in the town of Kielce, where forty-two returning survivors were killed by Poles. To say nothing, of course, of intense Communist anti-Semitism in the 1960s and the more recent feelings stirred up when conservative Catholics erected hundreds of crosses at the gates of Auschwitz. In March, 1999, the *New York Times* reported that the Polish government proposed to establish a 100-yard protection zone around the sites of former Nazi death camps to maintain a sense of dignity by prohibiting commercial development. Local residents immediately protested, saying that such a move would drive away investors. As stated in *The Real Guide—Poland*, "It's unnerving that anti-Semitism should remain a useful political tool in a country where virtually no Jews exist." I have been asked if I was surprised to learn that there were only five Jews still living in Bialystok. The big surprise to me is that there are between ten thousand and twenty-thousand Jews who have chosen to remain anywhere in the country known in Yiddish as Poylin.

Inside the apartment building, the chipped, stained walls of chilly hallways exuded stale aromas of fried onions and burned garlic. Now, at about ten thirty in the morning, we knocked at the door of what we hoped was the correct apartment, and another sleep-tousled man appeared, understandably annoyed. No, he is not a baker, he growls, and he knows of none in the building. Surely that drowsy man must have thought he was having a nightmare as two strange Poles and two even stranger Americans woke him to ask if he baked onion rolls.

In a further attempt to help me find bialys, Roman Powlowski patiently guided us to four grocery stores, in between pointing out a few sights, such as the famed clock tower of the Town Hall on Rynek Kosciuszko in the city center and the Branicki Palace with its spacious garden park, now the site of a medical academy. We passed the dilapidated Jewish Gymnasium where the ex-Israeli prime minister, Yitzak Shamir, had once been a student, and the totally wrecked Jewish cemetery, where lopsided, sinking headstones looked as though they might have been toppled by very restless souls beneath.

Finally, at the last shop on our tour, we found what I can only describe as a specimen that bore a passing resemblance to a bialy. It looked like a large, domed, moderately soft and shiny hamburger bun, topped with shreds of roasted onions, poppy seeds and, in the middle, a dab of melted yellow cheese. The shopkeeper gave us the name and telephone number of the baker, who turned out to be Francisek Rogalski, a gentile of about forty, who was too young to have known the original bialys. He explained that his parents told him that the Jews used to bake a small bread with onions and poppy seeds that everyone liked, and this was his interpretation. Perhaps his parents remembered something special going on in the center of that roll and, not knowing it was an indentation, the baker dabbed on cheese.

By that time—around one thirty—we were frozen and starved and, recognizing a dead end when we saw one, proceeded to lunch with Tomy Wisniewski. We met at what was considered the best restaurant in town, but when we arrived, a big rock band of musicians clad in black was rehearsing for the evening's performance, another surreal touch to this day. Conversation would have been impossible, and so we proceeded to the rather formal restaurant of the Hotel Cristal. At first we thought it was closed because it was so dark inside, but we were told by the manager that since only two tables were occupied, they would not turn on the lights.

We soon cast a glow of our own as we raised alternate toasts of *"L'chayim"* and *"Na'zdrowie"* with the premium vodka called Nissovka, or Passover, originally made of potatoes by Jews for the holiday that prohibits the use of fermented grain. Considered the purest vodka, Nissovka is prepared now in the traditional Jewish way by Poles who appreciate its quality. Along with Zybrowka, Nissovka fetches the highest price. As we were further revived by hot sauerkraut soup, creamed mushrooms, and the Polish mixed meat stew called bigos, I asked Tomy how, as a non-Jew, he became interested in the region's Jewish heritage. He explained that his interest in Jews and their fate began while he was jailed during the 1980s by the Communists for dissident activities. He was determined to find out more and to trace lost heritages, and so when he was freed, he did research on the Holocaust in Israel, Russia, Belarus, Lithuania, and the United States. In addition to editing, photographing, and writing, he and his wife, Iwona, now direct a Jewish genealogical service in the Bialystok region. He also has an outstanding collection of old postcards and photographs of that area.

Tomy gave me valuable leads to the library of the Yivo Institute in New York and told me of his meeting with Samuel Pisar, the renowned lawyer and native Bialystoker, whose autobiography, *Of Blood and Hope*, recounts his time in concentration camps and his life before and after the Holocaust and who also asked about the lost kuchen. Tomy described a meeting of Bialystokers that he attended in Israel, to which someone brought a huge bagful of the cherished rolls. He gave me the names of several at that meeting who might lead me to the source of those kuchen.

Our departure from the restaurant was even less felicitous than our dimly lit entry because I could not find our coat check. And though ours were the only two coats on the rack, it took about fifteen minutes of arguing to retrieve them from the checkroom bureaucrat.

Darkness fell early in Bialystok, and we realized that we had a long drive back to Warsaw through the nighttime mist and fog. We would be unable to pay our respects at the infamous concentration camp of Treblinka, about halfway between the two cities, or to visit other towns with Jewish memorials in the surrounding area, with their ruined cemeteries and fragments of the wooden houses the area was noted for. None of the region's famed wooden synagogues still exists. But we did stop for a few minutes at the Russian flea market in Bialystok, crowded despite the wet snow, where the array of merchandise ranged from mink and the highly prized Polish amber (the best having fossils within) to secondhand, dented pots and pans and huge, wide salamis that looked as though they had been run over by a truck.

Our only stop on the way back to Warsaw was in Tykocin, about 15 miles outside of Bialystok. Here Jews had first settled in 1522. In 1642, the old wooden Duza Synagogue was replaced with the baroque structure that is now a Jewish museum. Displayed in the big, square, airy space is a graceful wrought-iron eighteenth-century *bima*, or four-pillared altar, and lacy, candlelit chandeliers and wall cases of silver Judaica, such as Torah finials and pointers, Hanukkah lamps, seder plates, and kiddush cups, along with Passover Haggadahs and a handsome ark cover donated by the New

York Jewish community in 1981. Frescoes with gracefully lettered Hebrew prayer texts have been restored, and atop a small staircase near the synagogue entrance is a tower room with a re-creation of a seder table and a rabbi's study.

Luckily, the museum director, Ewa Wroczynska, was our gracious and informed guide. Like all of the other museum staff members we encountered throughout Poland, she was Catholic, and to qualify for work in these state institutions, she had been well-trained in the Jewish history of the region, as were so many other Polish Christians now in charge of Jewish historical sites. Mrs. Wroczynska generously played recordings of haunting liturgical music sung by a cantor with a voice much like Richard Tucker's and explained that though the museum's present collection is considered a rich one, it represents the smallest part of the treasures it held before being ransacked first by Bolsheviks and then by Nazis.

Although there are no vestiges of the markets in the old Jewish quarter around the synagogue, we did see a relic of a wooden house with a Star of David poignantly framed in a windowpane.

Shivering from disappointment as much as from the chilly air, I felt as though I had just been in a surreal dream, wandering in a strange gray city, cold and wet and clutching an onion roll that no one recognized. As we drove back to Warsaw, I was frustrated by what I had not found, yet encouraged by some of the clues Tomy Wisniewski suggested. It dawned on me that my search for the Bialystoker kuchen fressers had just begun. Janusz promised to keep looking for traces of bialys as he traveled around Poland and thought there might be such a bakery in Lublin.

When we left Roman Powlowski and Tomy Wisniewski, I gave them my two sample bialys, which Tomy described in Polish as *bialostockiej kuchni* or *bulki* in an article about my visit that appeared in *Kurier Poranny*. Perhaps the seeds of an idea were thus planted, for seven years later, Tomy faxed to tell me that little onion rolls have become available recently in Bialystok at a shop called, oddly enough, New York Bagels, where the round rolls, *bulki*, are baked with onions and poppy seeds. Tomy said that the owner of that bakery, Joann Pacewicz, knew of the Jewish kuchen baked there and tried to imitate them as best he could, but missing the defining center indentation. It is ironic that this near-bialy has come full circle to Bialystok and, perhaps even more so, that "New York" should be acknowledged as the imprimatur of authenticity. Much the same is true of the bagel, which undoubtedly also originated in Eastern Europe and which was a staple of the Polish Jewish diet for centuries before the Holocaust.

Because my side trip had no place in my article for the *Condé Nast Traveler*, I wrote about it for the English edition of the Jewish weekly newspaper *Forward*. In addition, I realized that the *Bialystoker Shtimme* would bring my search to the attention of many former Bialystokers living all over the world, especially since every article was printed in both English and Yiddish. After thanking Izaak Rybal for his help and telling him of my findings, I proposed a brief article for the *Shtimme* in which I would ask readers to share their memories of Bialystok and their lives after leaving that city and of the kuchen, including versions they might know of elsewhere in the world.

As the Bialystok Center is a charitable institution, I decided not to accept payment for the article, even if it was offered. I needn't have worried. Izaak Rybal's policy for placing articles in the *Shtimme* was one that I hope no other publishers adopt. Not only was payment not offered, but as soon as I asked to do the article, Rybal, without missing a beat, said, "You'll have to make a contribution."

"How much?" I asked.

"You tell me," he answered.

"One hundred dollars?" I offered.

After an expressive pause he replied, "Hm! It'll be all right. But when you see the beautiful job we will do with your story, you'll want to send more."

"Fine," I answered, then as an afterthought, "Of course, I want it to appear in both English and Yiddish."

"That'll cost you another hundred dollars," he shot back.

Having walked right into that one, I wrote a check to the Center for two hundred dollars.

It was money well spent because the article brought forth intriguing letters from Israel, France, Australia, Argentina, and the United States. Some were written in English, but others were in old-style Polish, Yiddish and Hebrew, and through the *Forward* I found several able translators. My donation also entitled me to a subscription to the *Shtimme*, from which I gathered many more names of former Bialystokers who were contributors. As I eventually learned, there were many prolific writers in that group, and they produced not only short pieces for the *Shtimme* but also autobiographies recounting their memories and their fate as Bialystok Jews, who, I was to discover, remain a closely knit group, albeit one that is far-flung.

T H E   S E M A N T I C S
A N D   O R A L   H I S T O R Y
O F   T H E   B I A L Y

Intermittently throughout my research, I have come up against the opinion that bialys were unknown in Bialystok and were, in fact, invented in New York.

One such school claims that the bialy was merely a pletzl, pure and simple. Clearly the forerunner of the bialy and made of the same dough by the same bakers, the pletzl is larger and, most critically, lacks the center well or indentation that defines the bialy. Others say that the bialy took its name from the prebaking dusting of white flour, *bialy* being the word for "white" in Slavic languages. But that ignores the fact that the roll was always identified by the city's name, which in turn is derived from the White River, or a *bialystok* in Polish, according to David I. Gold, a Yiddish and Hebrew linguist who taught at the University of Haifa and who is now back in the United States as director of the Jewish-English Archives.

In addition, as already stated, for at least a century, the Jews of Bialystok were nicknamed "Bialystoker kuchen fressers" by their neighbors. I contend that the difference is semantic and that what did not exist in Bialystok was simply the name, bialy. Although truly a bread, these rolls were known as kuchen or, more fondly and diminutively, as kuchelach, from the German word for cake. (In his collection of Jewish recipes and food culture, *Yiddish Cuisine*, Rabbi Robert Sternberg explains that *kuchen* in Yiddish means simply something that is baked.)

When they began to be baked in New York by émigrés from Bialystok, somewhere around 1920, judging from my interviews with present and former bialy bakers, the rolls were known as Bialystoker kuchen, a name soon shortened to bialys. As you will see throughout this book, the characteristic kuchen with its trademark center well has been recalled to me in the most explicit details, sometimes with drawings, by ex-Bialystokers in Israel, the United States, France, Australia, and Argentina. Several of those respondents who were more than ninety years old—and the oldest, the late Ben Halpern of Detroit who was 101 when I last interviewed him—remembered eating kuchen as well as the larger, flatter pletzls as children in Bialystok.

In addition, I also interviewed two descendants of Bialystokers who claim forebears said to have invented the famed kuchen, both in the latter part of the nineteenth century. Apocryphal as such claims might be, they leave little doubt that the bakers were producing kuchen, even if they did not invent them. Having traveled to Bialystok to trace her roots shortly after I visited the area, Nina Selin with her husband, Dr. Ivan Selin, then the Chairman of the Nuclear Regulatory Commission, heard about my search from Tomy Wisniewski, who was their guide as he had been mine. The Selins, who live in Washington, D.C., and who have become friends, called to tell me that Nina was a descendant of three generations of bialy bakers and that her maternal great-great grandfather, one Moshe Nosovich, born in 1835, was considered the inventor of the bialystoker kuchen (although Nina did not say considered by whom). Members of Nina's family recall their grandparents' talking of the bakery on Institute Street, now called Palace Street and in view of the *stadtzeiger*—Yiddish for "town clock." Ivan Selin added, "The family eventually had three bakeries and became so wealthy due to the success of the kuchen that they lived in a prosperous part of town and not over any of their stores."

Through the underground network of bialy contacts I developed, Roberta Russell Krieger of New York learned of my research. She called to tell me of her great-grandmother, Hadassah Ottenstein, an indomitable baker in Bialystok, who was born around 1850 and who lived to the age of ninety-four. In between having three children and at least as many husbands, she is also credited with the invention of the bialy.

Another generous respondent, Ruth Sobel, now about eighty and living in Riverdale, came to New York from Bialystok in 1938, when she was eighteen, and recalls going to buy kuchen fresh from the oven every morning. "I bought them from a baker on Zamenhof Street, known to Jews as Yatke Street because there were many butchers there, and in Yiddish, *yatke* is a butcher shop. The kuchen were about nine inches in diameter. Pletzls were bigger and were flat on top." Proud of being a graduate of Bialystok's prestigious Jewish high school, or gymnasium, Mrs. Sobel, who is fluent in Hebrew, taught that language for many years in the United States.

Finally, as a result of contacts made through my article in the *Forward*, I had a telephone interview with Irene Swillinger, who lives in Brooklyn and whose father Louis Kass (né Lebl Koussevitsky) baked bialys in Bialystok, until he emigrated to the Borough Park section of Brooklyn where, his daughter conjectures, he introduced bialys to the United States. By the time I spoke to Irene Swillinger, I had heard the surprising news that in Bialystok the kuchen were often eaten with the pressed sesame-seed candy, halvah. As much as I love this sweet and grainy fudgelike confection, I couldn't imagine it as a garnish for an onion roll. Irene said that she had heard of that combination, but that in her family, they ate halvah with a plain roll. When I asked her if that wasn't terribly dry, she answered, "We used to choke! But you know, it's not so very different from peanut butter."

Nothing would do but for me to taste it for myself, and Irene Swillinger was right. Choking is indeed a dangerous possibility. But even more, I could find nothing interesting or even distinctive about this strange concoction, with the flavor of the bialy and the halvah mutually resistant, each recognizable separately but never blending on the palate.

There is even visual proof of the bialy's existence in the documentary film *Jewish Life in Bialystok*, produced in the crucial year of 1939 and distributed by the National Center for Jewish Film. It clearly shows laughing children eating the kuchen that look almost exactly like today's bialys, although a bit larger and with a wider well.

In his moving account of the Holocaust and its aftermath, *A Hole in the Heart of the World,* Jonathan Kaufman states, "From food to prayer books, Polish Jews reshaped

Jewish life and set the standard that would follow their descendants to America. The bialy, which American Jews ate in New York and Los Angeles, originated in Bialystok, Poland."

Furthermore, no less an authority than Leo Rosten, the author and Yiddishist, in his classic book *The Joys of Yiddish*, describes the bialy's shape as being like a wading pool and adds, "The name is taken from the bakers of Bialystok, where this exquisite product was presumably perfected."

Then, his illustrative joke:

> *"Forty cents a dozen for bialies?" protested Mrs. Becker. "The baker across the street is asking only twenty!"*
>
> *"So buy them across the street."*
>
> *"Today, he happens to be sold out."*
>
> *"When I'm out of bialies, I charge only twenty cents a dozen, too."*

Information on the very word *bialy* came from the Yiddish linguist David I. Gold. As purists do, he regrets the use of German spellings and pronunciations for Yiddish words.

"Though Kossar's and others may use the German-based romanization 'bialystoker kuchen,'" Dr. Gold wrote, "it would be better to use the Yiddish, *byalestoker kukhn*. I have a slightly longer etymology for bialy, since I remember that another older name in English is Bialystok roll, now obsolete. I still write *byalestoker kukhn* hesitatingly and would prefer *byalestoker pletsl* [a pletzl with a center indentation], but if it was called a kukhn in Bialystok, so be it." (In the interest of clarity, I have tried to use the most familiar Yiddish spellings, if not the most scholarly.)

To further complicate matters, consider that two of my older respondents—Charles "Shleimeh" Zabuski in Paris and the late Max Ratner of Cleveland—referred to these rolls as bialystoker bagels. And, as I learned several years later in Israel, the word for bialy in Esperanto is *kuko*, according to Yerachmiel Giladi, a Bialystok émigré who is one of five hundred or so devoted Esperantists who gather regularly in Tel Aviv to speak the international language that was devised in Bialystok by Dr. Ludwik Zamenhof. Based on a combination of existing European languages, Esperanto (meaning "hope") was devised as the unifying tongue of a somewhat utopian one world.

The bialy's indentation may seem like a minor distinction between it and the flat-topped pletzl, but in culinary matters, many such tiny variations in form are the identifying features accounting for different names, however similar the ingredients. Prime examples of such culinary distinctions are Italian filled pastas such as cappelletti and tortellini, ravioli and agnolotti, all differing only in size and a twist or a curve here and there.

As with the origins of the bagel, the doughnut, pasta, and

many other preparations, it is doubtful that anyone will ever know unequivocally who first formed a bialystoker kuchen and when. My guess is that it originated by accident as a variation on the more ubiquitous pletzl that is still made by all bialy bakers. Given the random fickleness of fate, I conjecture that one day an unbaked pletzl fell onto a bakery floor and was stepped on with the heel of a shoe. Not wanting to waste anything, the frugal baker topped it with onions and poppy seeds, baked it, tasted it, and proclaimed a eureka moment in bread history.

That is the theory I shall have to content myself with until I find any evidence of the bialy's origins, anecdotal or scientifically irrefutable.

B I A L Y S   I N   A M E R I C A :   T H E   L A S T   S T R O N G H O L D   O F   A N   E N D A N G E R E D   S P E C I E S

As I began to receive bialy memoirs, I wanted to know more about how these humble onion rolls are made and how they evolved in the eighty or so years of their existence in New York and elsewhere around the United States. Danny Scheinin kindly let me hang around Kossar's and take notes. In the winter of 1998 he sold the bakery to Judah Engelmayer and Danny Cohen, two energetic, thirty-something brothers-in-law, who still follow the traditional methods for baking bialys and also uphold the custom of a baker's dozen that includes thirteen pieces.

I always love walking into Kossar's, a wide, bright store that, in an old-fashioned way, is really a bakery with a small, makeshift sales counter. The air is veiled in flour, and the scent of yeast, onions, and baking bread warmly engulf visitors. Silent bakers in white T-shirts work with professional assurance, rolling, kneading, shaping, smearing on onions, and taking baked bialys from the oven. Passersby on Grand Street peer through the big front windows, and shoppers idle in and out, schmoozing, making purchases, and usually, buying one extra bialy to be eaten out of hand.

Danny Scheinin explained that too often in the United States today, bialys and bagels are made in the same bakeries, both from the same bagel dough. But a true bialy requires much more yeast than do bagels, so that it will rise quickly and its rim will be gently soft. Also, bialys are made without the malt or sugar that is added to bagels to produce a golden crust, and unlike bagels, they are not boiled before being baked. (If authentic bialy bakeries sell bagels, they usually buy them from a bagel baker.)

For the most part, good bialys come from dedicated bialy bakeries, where the only other products are different shapes of bialy dough, such as bulkas—long, oval rolls topped with onions or garlic and poppy seeds—and pletzls that are ten-to-twelve-inch flat rounds, liberally sprinkled with poppy seeds and onions.

Kossar's bialy dough is made authentically with only four ingredients: high-gluten flour, salt, ice water, and bakers' yeast. Forget about sugar, eggs, or oil, all of which are recommended in various cookbooks. Kossar's recipe for a dough batch that makes seventy to eighty dozen bialys, includes 100 pounds of high-gluten flour, 7 gallons of ice water, 2 pounds of salt, and about 1 pound of yeast, depending on the weather, more yeast being necessary on colder days. Until early 2000, the mixing and shaping went as follows: These ingredients were quickly, briefly combined in a huge commercial electric mixer and allowed to rise in the mixer bowl for two to three hours, or until the dough began to come together but was still very sticky. The dough was then turned out on a lightly floured board and divided into about nine 6-pound mounds. Each was kneaded by hand, that step being impossible with older machines because the dough was so sticky.

Next, the shaping began. With an experienced eye and hand, the bakers divided the large mounds of dough into roughly thirty smaller balls, each weighing about three ounces to make bialys that are four inches in diameter. After rising for one hour, each ball was lightly rolled between the baker's floured palms and was then gently flattened onto a board. Now the mixing, kneading, and balling are done by machine, with barely noticeable differences in the final results.

Forming the identifying center indentation is still done by hand. Working at lightning speed, the bakers shape the center well by placing both thumbs on top of the center of each round of dough, with their index and middle fingers underneath. They then press and slightly stretch the dough to form the well. Invited to try my hand, I found the ball of gentle dough almost cuddly to work with, and so delicate that if I pressed my thumb against my fingers too firmly, I tore through the dough. After struggling to shape about six bialys, I gained much respect for the bakers like Whitey Aquanno, who has been at Kossar's since 1973 and who forms the wells with almost invisible motions at a dazzling rate.

This hand method of shaping is relatively new to bialy baking, as the well used to be impressed with a small rolling pin. Danny Scheinin recalls that in 1956, when he joined the bakery, his father-in-law, Morris Kossar, bought the wooden rolling pins used in Orthodox communities for making Passover matzohs. Such matzoh baking is done only from January to Passover, and since each year's rolling pins have to be new, the used ones must be discarded or sold cheaply. Bakery owners used to cut the longer pins into the two- to three-inch lengths they required, or as an alternative, they ordered small rolling pins from neighborhood carpenters. The traditional rolling pin used for bialys in Bialystok had two thin rod handles and a thicker center cylinder, so that the center of the bialy would be depressed while the rim remained high. That rolling pin closely resembled the type still used for making dim sum in China.

Saving time is one reason for the switch from rolling pin to hands. In addition, according to Danny Scheinin, the brick-lined gas ovens that replaced the old coal- and wood-fired ovens bake so rapidly that the compressed, thick dough formed by a rolling pin cannot bake thoroughly before the onions and the top crusts burn.

I agree with those who insist that the rolling pins pro duced a more tantalizing texture, with a firmer, densely packed, and crackly center. As skillful as a baker may be, even at Kossar's, the center wells are not always compressed enough and so rise in the oven, leaving little or, sometimes, no indentation.

Thus formed, the bialys are ready for the topping of onions (and poppy seeds when they were used). In the best of all possible worlds, the onions will be large, white, and sweet and will be chopped by hand, not ground by a meat grinder. Understandably, in commercial bakeries, grinding is more practical. To absorb the water in the onions, Kossar's grinds seven- or eight-hour-old bialys (hard but not stale) into crumbs and mixes them with the onions (one bialy to ten onions) to achieve a spreadable mixture much like wet sand. The onions should be ground no more than two days in advance of use. Freezing them to ensure a steady supply is understandable for a high-volume bakery, but some flavor and aroma will be lost. In any case, the onions should be absolutely raw, never sautéed, steamed, or salted down, despite such instructions in many cookbooks. A common practice in many bialy bakeries is to use dehydrated onions that tend to burn into acrid, black flecks unless they are first soaked in water, in which case, they generally turn unpleasantly pink and have a stale, metallic flavor. I found that all garlic used in bialy bakeries, including Kossar's, is dehydrated or freeze-dried and, therefore, tastes stale and unpleasantly acidic.

The onion mixture is quickly smeared by hand into the well and on top of each shaped, unbaked bialy. The kuchen are all then placed on big wooden peels and slid onto the revolving iron shelves of a brick-lined, 500-degree gas oven. Undoubtedly old-timers are right in their claims that bialys had a more richly burnished, smokier flavor when baked in a wood-fired oven.

Now, another choice is necessary. Obviously, the longer the bialys bake, the darker brown and crispier they will be. As someone who likes very well-done bialys with nice dark brown blistered tops and crisp toasted bottoms, I find myself increasingly frustrated by the mostly whiter and softer bialys sold today. The choice appears to be generational. Customers over fifty-five or sixty generally choose the dark rolls, while the younger customers prefer the light. Danny Cohen and Judah Engelmayer, Kossar's new owners, also prefer the light bialys and caution their bakers to stop "burning" them. They feel, probably correctly, that the lighter ones keep longer and also that the younger clientele they must attract shares their preference. Recently they must have reconsidered, because they now always seem to have a batch or two of the crisp, dark-brown beauties that I cherish.

Fortunately, what I consider underbaked bialys can be finished off at home, just before they are served. That is a practical step anyway, since I buy a dozen or two at a time, slice them through the middle, wrap each in foil and freeze them. I then bake them, still wrapped, in a 500-degree oven until they thaw. Then I unwrap them, open them to expose the cut sides, and bake them for another five to seven minutes, until the crust becomes brown and crisp and the tops just a bit firm.

Please remember that there is a difference between an oven-heated bialy and one that is toasted, meaning that it is split and placed directly under a broiler flame or toaster-oven grill. (It's a mistake to put a bialy in a toaster, as the onions will surely burn.) Toasting is as antithetical to the true spirit of the bialy as it is to the bagel and belongs more to the aesthetics of the English muffin. Five or six years after I began my research, I spoke to Pauline Rabin, who has a long family history in the bialy business as the proprietor of New York Bagels 'n Bialys, now in Scottsdale, Arizona, by way of the Bronx and Chicago. She told me that some of her customers like big bialys, but that "real New Yorkers" do not want them larger than three-and-a-half inches because they will not fit into a toaster. "New Yorkers have to toast everything!" she said with obvious disgust. It is among the most disappointing observations I have ever heard about my *landsleit*, but then, they are New Yorkers who moved to Arizona.

Another difference in the buying habits of old- and new-timers is the degree of freshness they demand. In Bialystok, and here too with those over sixty, the only good bialys were those right from the oven. Shoppers waited in line, by-passing baskets full of bialys that might have come from the oven just fifteen minutes earlier, to wait for the next, hot batch. Modern life has altered this habit somewhat, since bialy bakeries are not usually within a short distance of all homes, and busier families buy bialys in bulk and freeze them. It is therefore less critical that one sees the bialys issuing forth from the oven. However, chewing on a hot, freshly baked bialy is an incomparable joy, what with the mingling scents of yeast and onions, the teasing textural contrast of crisp crust and the puffy softness of the rim and the cozy warmth in the hand, especially on a cold winter day. (When buying hot bialys, make sure that they are not enclosed in plastic bags, as they will steam and turn limp. A loosely closed paper bag is the correct wrapping.)

Deciding how to eat the bialy is the next delightful step. Much to my amazement, I learned early on in my research that I had always been eating them the "wrong" way and, in fact, still do. Like most Americans, I slice each bialy horizontally through the middle, to form a sandwich, bagel-style. But as I learned from ex-Bialystokers, the roll was never sliced through, even when smeared with butter or soft white cheese. Such spreads went either on the bottom or over the top of the uncut roll. If underneath, one took care not to shake loose the onions and especially the poppy seeds; if over the top, a little extra spread was stuffed into the well to form an especially luscious mouthful. When I discussed this custom with Gloria Kossar Scheinin, a woman steeped in bialy culture, first as the daughter of Morris Kossar, then as the wife of Danny Scheinin, I expected her to share my surprise. "Who slices a bialy?" she asked. "It's not a roll, you know."

Although I value authenticity, I must admit that, while uncut bialys without any spread are especially satisfying to chew, especially with a cup of hot coffee, I find it awkward to eat them with cheese or butter on the outside, and there is no graceful way to include a slice of smoked salmon or of the silky smoked cod called sable, or a scrambled egg without making a sandwich.

Of the few changes bialys have gone through after their voyage to America none is more striking or inexplicable than the disappearance of poppy seeds. Along with the slivers of roasted onions, those tiny round gray-black seeds—the beloved *mohn*—was the feature most fervently recalled by every former Bialystoker I interviewed. In the United States, poppy seeds are sprinkled onto garlic bialys, but when that practice began remains a mystery. Neither Danny Scheinin nor anyone else I spoke with recalls ever seeing poppy seeds on onion bialys in this country.

Poppy seeds are used liberally on untraditional garlic bialys, as well as on pletzls and bulkas in most of these shops, but according to Scheinin and others in the business, the seeds are put onto garlic bialys to differentiate them from those with onions, as an aid to salespeople. The obvious question seemed to be, "Why not put the poppy seeds on the onion bialys instead? They would still look different and the poppy seeds would be where they belong." For the most part, I was answered with a shrug and a mumble, until one day a really convincing answer emerged.

"Poppy seeds are very expensive," said Eddie Ebert, a partner in several Slim's Bagel and Bialy bakeries in Queens and Nassau County. "We sell twenty onion bialys to every one with garlic, so it's cheaper to identify the garlic with the seeds." He might also have added that because these seeds contain oil, they become rancid and take on the stale, musty flavor that often ruins pletzls and poppy-seed-filled pastries such as strudel, coffee cakes, and hamentaschen, the three-cornered turnovers traditional for the Purim holiday.

Luckily for lovers of traditional bialys, Engelmayer and Cohen have made few changes in that classic, even though the preparation is a bit more automated. In an effort to simpify production, they no longer make a four-inch bialy for their wholesale trade and a three-inch for retail but bake the larger size exclusively, with only a very slight price increase. They are also trying nontraditional variations of the same dough, including garlic knots—long, chunky, gar-lic-topped rolls with a knot tied at each end—and the sesame-encrusted thin bulkas that they call sticks, much favored by Chinese customers now moving into the Lower East Side.

Their best addition is the mini-onion disk, really a six-inch pletzl that is generously strewn with poppy seeds and onions to give it a tantalizing crunch. They have also opened Kossar's Bagelry & Catering, a small take-out food shop and luncheonette on Essex Street, just around the corner from the original bakery, where they serve bagels and bialys with smoked-fish and cream-cheese spreads, freshly cooked egg dishes, and good, if hefty, homemade muffins. There they also bake delicious, if overly large, bagels from a separate dough prepared at the original Kossar's. They are hoping to get enough production to make pizzas, for, as observed by their Italian baker, Whitey Aquanno, the doughs are almost identical. "Italians used to be some of the best bialy bakers," Judah Engelmayer said, "but they don't go into that work anymore, and now we are finding that some of the new Russian immigrants have a talent for it, too."

A few changes, which don't actually affect the bialy's flavor, took place because Kossar's new owners, themselves Orthodox Jews, want to enlarge their market by offering kosher bialys. They are glatt kosher, which in general usage means that they are superkosher and so are *shomer shabbes*—Sabbath observers who close the bakery from sundown Friday until sundown Saturday, as well as during Passover week and on many other Jewish holidays. Otherwise they maintain the Kossar tradition of remaining open twenty-four hours a day.

According to Rabbi Daniel Alder of the Brotherhood Synagogue on Gramercy Park in New York, "glatt" in the strictest, technical sense applies only to meat. When an animal is slaughtered, its organs and especially the lungs are examined by a *bodek*, or inspector, for blemishes. If there is a small scratch but no tumor or infection on the lung's lining, the meat of the animal is considered kosher. For it to be glatt, it must be completely unblemished and smooth, the meaning of glatt in Yiddish. Rabbi Alder said that in wider, more general use, glatt has come to signify extra diligence in observing all aspects of kashrut.

Danny Scheinin told me that an Orthodox rabbi once suggested he make his bakery glatt kosher to attract more customers. When Danny said that he did not want to bother, he was rabbinically advised to sell the bakery to a gentile every Friday afternoon and buy it back every Saturday evening. Not only would that maneuver have created an interesting income tax return for the entrepreneurial *shabbes goy* (a gentile paid to perform the tasks forbidden to Jews on the Sabbath), but members of the local Orthodox community, who tend to know exactly what is going on around them, wouldn't have been fooled at all.

The same rabbi further noted that for the bakery's products to be truly kosher, it would be necessary to sacrifice a portion of each batch of unbaked dough by burning it in the oven, a ritual known as "separating challah." ("Challah" here has the Hebrew meaning of "the priest's portion," as described in the Old Testament, Numbers 15:20 and Ezekiel 44:30.) However, the rabbi continued, if 51 percent of the liquid used in the dough is apple juice instead of water, the bialys would officially, talmudically, be designated cake, not bread (because of the sugar in the juice), and so it would be unneccesary to sacrifice dough.

Kossar's new owners wisely rejected the apple-juice

option, for in thus saving the need to sacrifice dough, they surely would have sacrificed the bialy's true flavor and texture. Judah Engelmayer and Danny Cohen make the ritual sacrifice with roughly 2 to 3 percent of each batch of dough. The daily supply of bialy dough is prepared around four thirty in the morning, when a *broche* (prayer) must be said by an Orthodox Jew. As such an early hour would be difficult for the new owners, who have both kept their day jobs (Danny Cohen as an investment banker and Judah Engelmayer as executive assistant to New York State Comptroller, H. Carl McCall), an Orthodox baker who works for the nearby kosher pastry shop, Gertel's, stops by on his way to work and performs the ceremony.

To see just how complex this ritual can get, consider that no pleasure may be realized from that sacrificial portion, for self-denial is really the point. Because Cohen and Engelmayer fear that by baking that sacrificial dough together with bialys in the same oven, some crumbs might attach to one of the finished rolls and so accidentally be enjoyed, they save the batches of sacrificial dough all week and, before closing on Friday, burn them in the otherwise empty oven and discard the remains.

However complicated, their changes seem to be working for them. The twelve hundred or so dozen bialys sold each day under Danny Scheinin's watch have now increased to sixteen hundred dozen, of which some eight hundred are sold at retail in their own store and the rest at wholesale. They also sell all over the country through their website (see page 151).

Internet shopping for bialys may be the only option open to those far from New York, but it hardly compares with the human experience of going into Kossar's on Saturday at midnight or later, as bearded Orthodox Jews line up for bialys along with the purple- and green-haired young swingers who drop by after a night at the new, hip clubs now opening around nearby Ludlow Street.

If the future seems relatively safe for bialy purists in Manhattan at Kossar's, I did not find it to be so elsewhere in the New York area. Traveling to Brooklyn to try the specimens turned out by Bell Bagels and Bialys in Canarsie and the Coney Island Bagel Bakery on Coney Island Avenue, I found those, like others from Slim's in Queens and Nassau County, to be pale, strangely damp and rubbery, and topped with at least some of the dismal flesh-pink onions.

And even in Manhattan, Millie Graves, "the Bialy Lady" who is a renegade from the world of high fashion, has been creating designer bialys that she has sold wholesale for the past seven or eight years. Her bialys are much larger than the standards, and are topped with various vegetables and herbs, or nothing at all, not even onions, and some are made of wholewheat flour, for a heavy, grainy effect. She also turns out other shapes from her bialy dough, including a sort of pita pocket. Having tasted them intermittently through the years, I find them mildly pleasant as bread, but not worthy of the bialy accolade.

Beyond New York, matters are even worse, a statement I make confidently after having sampled bialys from Miami Beach and elsewhere in Florida, and from Chicago, Scottsdale, and Beverly Hills. All seemed underbaked and undersalted and, in addition to onions or garlic, might be made with blueberries or even raisins and cinnamon sugar. Weirdest of all is one I picked up at the Broadway Deli in Santa Monica, a huge albinotic, floppy disk of almost raw dough smeared with glassy white squares of onions that looked bleached.

Nor do California bialys hold any charms for Meyer Galler, a food technologist who was born in Bialystok and loved kuchen as a child and who spent ten years in a Soviet gulag, where he wrote three volumes on Russian prison slang. Now living close to Berkeley, the eighty-four-year-old Galler reports, "The kuchen was the symbol of Bialystok and there they were hard and crisp. But in California they are soft and white."

I must admit some responsibility for maverick bialys

being created in Austin, Texas. There my good friend, Patricia Slate, the gifted cook and baker who owns the delectable Sweetish Hill Bakery, heard me rant about bialys and thought they might be novelties for her loyal breakfast clientele. And so she came to New York, where Danny Scheinin and his bakers walked her through their methods, even giving her their recipe, which she faithfully mastered.

Unfortunately, what appeals to New Yorkers can fall flat with Texans. Trying to be more authentic than Kossar's, Patricia Slate topped her bialys with poppy seeds, only to find that Texans wouldn't touch them; they also complained that the onions got stuck in their toasters. Some locals rejected the flavor of onions at breakfast but, surprisingly, loved garlic and bits of jalapeño peppers that were stirred into some of the dough for an interesting fusion flavor. In addition, like the young Wonder Bread set in New York, Lone Star bialy eaters prefer those that are very lightly baked and pale, and they spread them with strawberry cream cheese as well as with the more suitable salmon and herb spreads. Patricia Slate reported that they also had trouble pronouncing bialy in the early days and tended to call them "bee-lees" and "bay-lees," and many just called them bagels.

Strange that this should all take place in Austin, where a secret bialy maven was long in residence.

Photograph by Yasushi Egami.

——————

FIVE

CASTING BIALYS ON
THE WATERS

As I did research during 1993, the year following my visit to Bialystok, I realized that I knew much about the bialy's current status in New York, but I wanted to learn more about its past in this city and how it has fared around the country.

Austin was to figure large in my research, because of the presence there of Roy M. Mersky, whose father was one of the founders of Mirsky & Kossar's. His was the first letter I received after my article appeared in the *Forward*. The Director of Research at the Tarlton Law Library at the Jamail Center for Legal Research, University of Texas at Austin, Roy Mersky said that in the 1930s and 1940s, his father, Irving Mirsky, a Russian immigrant, became the partner in several bialy bakeries in New York. (Roy Mersky's name is spelled with an *e* instead of an *i* because of an error made in his high-school records.) Morris Kossar, a young baker who began to work for him in 1927, eventually bought out other partners, and from 1936 to 1953, they owned Mirsky & Kossar, to become Kossar's when Mirsky left to open a small delicatessen in upstate New York.

Roy Mersky explained that his father's first name was originally Isadore, precisely the example used by Leo Rosten in *The Joys of Yiddish*. Writes Rosten, "In the 1920s and 1930s, many Jews altered first names as a step toward assimilation." As typical examples he cites, "Isadore to Irving and later to Erving . . . and Morris to Maurice." Morris Kossar has been referred to as Murray by several people I interviewed, but to his credit, he probably couldn't make the leap to Maurice.

About two years after our correspondence, I went to Austin on an assignment for *New Woman* magazine and the first thing I did was to have dinner with Roy Mersky. Looking for all the world like a lifelong Texan—trim, and impeccably dapper in blue jeans, denim jacket, and plaid shirt held by a leather bolo tie—he appeared a far cry from what I expected after reading his first letter. Between conversations on that visit and later ones by telephone, he recalled much about his days in New York, helping out at the bakery.

"I recall my father talking about delivering bialys with a

horse and wagon before the nineteen thirties in Manhattan. He always had a partner," Roy began. "One man handled the baking, and the other, my father, was responsible for the deliveries. As a young boy in high school, I would go down to the Lower East Side on Sundays and help him deliver the bialys to restaurants and retail stores. I would sit in the truck backwards on a box, where the passenger seat would have been.

"There were three people on the truck: One drove, one counted, and the third person stood on the running board, jumping off and dropping off the hot bialys. I was the counter. The bialys actually were hot, just out of the oven. They were in big wicker laundry baskets with two handles, and I would put them into bags—two dozen, three dozen, or a dozen and a half. I would hand the bag to the person riding the running board. I sat there surrounded by the strong onion aroma that was so pervasive, it frequently nauseated me, especially since I rode backwards.

"My father had everything in his head; he used no records, no adding machine, no paper, no anything. But every time we came to a restaurant, he would know just how many dozen bialys that customer ordered. I don't even remember invoices being given to those customers. Every Friday my father collected the money in cash.

"The baking was done Sunday through Thursday. There would be no baking on Friday and Saturday, as the bakery closed from sundown Friday through all day Saturday in observance of the Sabbath. However, the ovens would be fired up on Saturday night, so that fresh bialys would be ready as the sun rose on Sunday morning.

"The bialy bakeries were always in the basements of tenement houses. I remember them on Clinton, Essex, Hester, and Orchard Streets. I never visited one in Brooklyn, but I did see one somewhere in the East Bronx."

Remembering retail customers coming to the bakery to buy two or three bialys at a time, Roy Mersky reiterated that they would wait for those coming out of the oven no matter how many were ready in baskets. He also recalled that the bakeries closed during Passover, when bread cannot be eaten by observant Jews. Then all the bagel and bialy bakers would go to the Catskills for a week-long vacation.

"Bagels constituted the big industry and bialys were step-children," Roy continued. "They were not famous, and when I went off to the University of Wisconsin and people asked me what my father did, I couldn't say that he made bialys because no one would know what I was talking about. Instead, I said that he made Jewish novelty bakery products."

Having stayed in touch through the years, I was able to introduce Roy to my bialy contacts in Melbourne, Australia, when he went there for a seminar, and they invited him home for a Friday night Sabbath dinner. He has also been a reliable reporter on the progress being made by Patricia Slate in her continuing efforts to make bialy eaters of the students, writers, editors, film-makers, and pols in that university town and state capital. At last reports, the specimens Roy tried were somewhat underbaked and lacking in salt, to say nothing of the total absence of onions.

"Call my cousin, Arthur Boatin, who also used to work at the bakery," Roy Mersky suggested, and so I did.

"I started working at Mirsky & Kossar as a stranger in New York," the sixty-two-year-old Boatin said from his home in Maine. "My mother, Jessie Mendelson, and Roy's mother were sisters, but my father, Paul Boattini, who is now eighty-nine, came from Emilia-Romagna in Italy. I grew up in the Midwest, and when my parents divorced in 1948, I went to New York with my mother. We had very little money, and my Uncle Irving helped us a lot and gave me a weekend job at the bakery. I traveled down from the Bronx, and Murray Kossar drove me home. I remember that he had a big space between his front teeth and didn't talk much."

Besides being the counter on the delivery truck, Arthur Boatin also worked in the bakery and waited on retail customers; he also mentioned the demand for bialys right out of the oven. He still recalls eating plenty of bialys while on the job and that his uncle knew many details of his customers' lives and told a little story about each one as they made their rounds. He was also astounded that bialys would not be stolen when they were left at the doors of still unopened stores and restaurants before dawn.

"I liked being in the bakery where workers were dressed all in white and wore funny white hats on the backs of their heads—not yarmulkes, but sort of round hats that were flat on top and were made of either white paper or cloth. Not all of them were Jews. I remember one Italian man named Romolo. I loved the smell of the freshly chopped onions and the yeast as the dough rose, and I liked to watch the bakers use the little rolling pins to form the bialy centers. Coming from the Midwest, I was at first depressed by the Lower East Side, which seemed so drab and confusing and gray, but I got to love it and thought it was exotic. And I liked being the only kid working with adults."

Now semiretired as an editor, writer, teacher, and student advisor, Arthur Boatin said that he still bakes bread, even though he does no other cooking. Like his cousin Roy Mersky, Arthur Boatin recalled Slim Schwartzberg, the fastest "baller" in the business, his specialty being to form the individual rounds of dough and shape them into bialys.

Slim Schwartzberg proved elusive, and though several people knew that he was somewhere in Florida, none knew where or even his real first name. I eventually learned that his family still owned part of Slim's Bagel and Bialy Bakeries in Queens and Nassau County, and so I called Edward Ebert, a partner in those stores. He told me that the eighty-two-year-old Hyman or Slim Schwartzberg lives in Pembroke Pines, Florida, where he has been retired for the past twenty-five years. Slim still likes to drop into one of the three "Bagelmania" stores in Florida that are run by his son Gary. Another son, Jeffrey, has two successful Bagelmania stores in Santa Fe but found there was no local love for bialys, and so he discontinued them, much to his own regret. "I miss eating them myself," said Jeffrey, who was born in Brooklyn about fifty-five years ago. Besides Jeffrey's two shops, with their interest in the two bagel and bialy bakeries on Long Island, the family now has five bakeries in all, and grandsons have already joined them.

"It didn't happen overnight," Slim Schwartzberg assured me in a telephone interview as he warmed to what is obviously his favorite topic. "I began working in a bialy bakery—the one that became Mirsky & Kossar—in 1929, when I was eleven. It was at 22 Ridge Street on the Lower East Side, and I lived across the street, at number 35. I wanted a warm place to sleep because our apartment was cold, even though we had big eiderdown coverlets that my parents brought with them from Lublin. The bosses at the bakery said that if I carried in the coal and wood for the ovens, I could sleep on top of the flour sacks, near the ovens that were always hot. I loved sleeping there with the smell of burning wood and yeast."

Acknowledging his reputation as the fastest "baller" in the business, Schwartzberg said that he could shape ninety dozen, or 1,080, bialys an hour, and he did not need a scale to have every ball weigh exactly the right amount. "When we worked alone in the bakery at night, the bakers would send me out to Grand Street for coffee and I would get a dollar tip from the group.

"I also made extra money on Fridays, because the bakery closed at seven A.M. and didn't open until Saturday at five thirty P.M. I kept the ovens warm, and on Friday, Orthodox women in the neighborhood who were not allowed to cook over *shabbes* would bring their pots of cholent to be baked in the ovens, and I charged them twenty-five cents each. I could do that because I was not as strictly religious as they were."

Slim Schwartzberg explained that the next morning, just before lunchtime, the women would pick up the finished cholent—a baked casserole of meat, potatoes, barley, beans, onions, carrots, and other root vegetables.

"It was a wonderful place and always warm. When there was snow on the streets, it would melt on the sidewalk around the bakery where the steam rose. The ovens had brick walls a foot and a half thick floor to ceiling, and flames would shoot all the way up, making delicious crusts. We started the ovens with wood and then added coal."

As Slim Schwartzberg recalls, the bakery was begun about ten years before he started working there—about 1919 or 1920—by five men from Poland and Russia whose names he remembers as Max Gilbert, Meyer Gold, Nathan Perelstein, Zelig Shepps, and Isadore Mirsky. Slim also mentioned Morris Kossar, a worker in that bakery, who was formerly a cooper in Eastern Europe.

"We bialy bakers formed our own union, separate from the bread or bagel bakers, and I was the first delegate and remained one for five years," he says proudly. "I went into my own business in 1948 with Slim's in Jamaica, Queens."

Bagels are also baked at Bagelmania and are made with a different dough than the bialys. "For bialys, we used to let the dough rise for two hours for good flavor, and I would go out to a movie or something," he said. "We can't do that anymore because of the high cost of labor, so we use more yeast to make the dough rise faster.

"I go to one of our bakeries now and then and make a sort of bialy-pletzl for myself—a big round one with poppy seeds and freshly chopped onions that I salt first so the water will be drawn out of them. I cut the baked rounds in pieces when we have a party."

Gary Schwartzberg, forty-six, who runs the family

business, says that he has had experience since infancy, growing up around bialy bakeries in New York. "If you wanted to see my father, that's where you went."

When his father retired at about fifty-seven, he began to get lonesome in New York, and he followed Gary, who had moved to Fort Lauderdale, Florida, around 1977.

"There are so many Jews from New York down here that we have grown substantially," Gary said. "We still do almost traditional bialys, but others don't. When people leave their roots, the bialys and bagels change. Real old-timers, like my father and brothers and me, along with our sons and nephews, use just about the same formulas we always did. But the public taste has gone soft. At retail, old-timers who sometimes call them kuchen, want bialys that are baked dark but not burned. In supermarkets and restaurants, they want them light, so they can be toasted.

"A real true New Yorker does not toast bialys. But if you want to try something delicious, split the bialy and put butter on the cut sides, then slide it under a broiler for three or four minutes. My grandmother buttered her bialys upside down and I thought she was just too lazy to cut them.

"Onion bialys still sell best. That to us is a plain bialy. We make garlic regularly but will do plain or whole wheat or cinnamon-raisin mainly to order. My father was a great innovator in this business, and when he opened his own places in the nineteen forties and fifties, he began to make garlic bialys and to sell to supermarkets. We have a federal trademark for a biagel—bialy dough in a bagel shape that is baked but not boiled." He explained that they use fresh onions for the bialys they sell at retail but dried onions for those packaged for supermarkets and restaurants, because fresh onions have a short shelflife.

Gary Schwartzberg sent me some of his Florida bialys via Federal Express, including both the new and the traditional types. Although the traditional specimens were closer to New York's than others I eventually tried from sources around the country, they were worlds apart from Kossar's. The inner bread dough was thick, puffy and cream-colored, much like the modern bagels made with bromated flour, and there was absolutely no trace of crispness. The traditional type were loaded with the pink onion flecks I dislike, but the new had fewer of those offending onions and so were better. Oddly enough, although the out-of-town bialys all lacked texture and solid flavor, their form, with wide, flat centers, were closer to the Bialystok originals than Kossar's, where the well is less clearly defined.

It took only a few telephone conversations for me to locate another bialy expert, Pauline Rabin in Scottsdale, Arizona, where she operates the bakery New York Bagels 'n Bialys. In several telephone interviews, and between waiting on customers, she told me about her family's history in the business. By 1928, when she was born in the Bronx, her uncle, Benny Zuckerman, a baker from Bialystok, and her Russian father, Julius Cohen, were turning out bialys in a typical cellar bakery and delivering by horse and wagon. Eventually they graduated to what Pauline describes as "two sophisticated street-level shops" along Jerome Avenue. They also opened a store in South Fallsburg, New York, when many of their winter customers went to Catskill mountain *kochalayns*—literally, "cook alones," the one-room-with-kitchenette accommodations found in summer resorts.

That Pauline and her Brooklyn-born husband, Martin, spread the bialy gospel westward is a result of the labor movement. Bialy bakers' unions determined where bakeries could be opened. In the late 1960s, as the Bronx deteriorated, Pauline's family lived in Queens and wanted to move their business there but could not get union permission, even though her father had been a delegate.

"So in 1968 we moved to Chicago and opened New York Bagels 'n Bialys in Lincolnwood," she said. "And you know what? One year later the union dissolved. But we were settled in a house and had already established a good business, so we decided not to go back. Twenty years later, we sold that business. It's still there, with the same name, but we have no connection. We moved west again to Arizona and made Scottsdale a bialy town. Bagels are in our store name, of course, and we make good ones, but bialys are what we're famous for. We use the true bialy dough and fresh onions, although we use dehydrated onions on some of our other things.

"Now there are no more bialy unions and practically no craftsmen either, because you really had to know your stuff to get into the union. [Actually, bialy workers in New York now belong to Local 3, the Bread, Cake and Confectioners' Union, located in Long Island City.] My husband Martin learned the trade from my father and uncle after the Second World War, when his family went out of the smoking-pipe business. Now he's a great creator of new shapes, like our bialy sticks, and he really knows how to work with the dough. We had a lot to learn. The temperature here in Arizona sometimes goes to a hundred and ten or a hundred and twenty degrees, and that makes the yeast act much more rapidly."

Of the seven thousand or so bialys she sells each week, Pauline said that in addition to the onion, she makes oat bran, pumpernickel, jalapeño, garlic, and a best seller, cinnamon-raisin. Three and a half ounces of dough goes into each four-inch bialy, making it fairly large.

"Did you know bialys are the healthiest bread you can

eat?" Pauline asked rhetorically. Bialys have no malt like bagels and absolutely no sugar or any fat or oil.

As to color, Pauline said that New Yorkers always want their bialys baked brown, but Arizonans prefer them light. When I told her that these days even New Yorkers under fifty want them light, she said, "See? They don't know!"

Pauline and Martin Rabin generously shipped me some of their onion bialys, but alas, they were too large and doughy and not at all crisp, and I was put off by the damp, pink flecks of onion. However, they were better than those I had in Santa Monica, although a long way off from New York's.

SIX

LOOKING BACK AT BIALYSTOK
FROM AMERICA

Having found out much about the past and current state of bialys in America, I wanted to dig deeper into their history and learn more about them on their native ground. Oddly enough, none of the bialy bakers I spoke to in the United States had come from Bialystok, nor had their parents in most cases, and so they knew little about the original kuchen and the culture surrounding them. Thus, intermittently through the years, I searched for Bialystokers all over the world, hoping that they would share their memories of the kuchen and of how they were made and eaten. I found many through the *Bialystoker Shtimme*, most especially Leo Melamed in

Chicago, Max Ratner in Cleveland, and Sam Solasz in New York.

I figured that Leo Melamed might be a hard man to meet. I had seen him several times on CNN, when he commented on one financial crisis or another, and learned that he was a self-made financial wizard who earned his reputation in the commodity-futures markets. He is Chairman Emeritus and Senior Policy Advisor of the Chicago Mercantile Exchange, the Chairman and CEO of the global-futures firm of Sakura-Dellsher, and the man who had conceived and inaugurated the International Money Market, which allows for trading futures in gold and world currencies. This accomplishment prompted his friend and colleague, the Nobel Laureate economist Milton Friedman to say, "Almost single-handedly he transformed a minor commodity exchange into the leading futures market in the world. His influence was and remains worldwide." Of Leo Melamed's many credits, none ranked higher with me than his being a Bialystoker.

I was given his home telephone number by a secretary at the *Shtimme*, and so I was lucky enough to speak to his wife, Betty, and to try to make her my advocate. Friendly and forthcoming, she told me that, indeed, Leo loved Bialystoker kuchen and bought them in Chicago or brought them (with sour pickles) back from New York. She was sure he would talk to me and promised to speak to him and his secretary, so that I could get an appointment.

Although that sounded easy, I actually had to wait more than a year to pin down a date. I arrived in his reception room on April 13, 1995, at the appointed hour of three-thirty in the afternoon. Because I then had to wait an hour and a half to see Leo Melamed, I had plenty of time to admire the sleek, sweeping modern design of this room atop one of the glassy office towers in Chicago's financial district, and to read almost every magazine, and to stew.

Standing at his desk against shelves lined with sculptures, awards, art work, and family photographs, Leo Melamed exploded by way of greeting: "I don't know who you are, or what you want, or why I am seeing you." By that time, my temper was almost as short as his, but I couldn't help laughing, both at his candor and his resemblance to the curmudgeonly pianist-raconteur, the late Oscar Levant.

I launched into my credentials as a food critic and journalist, named every book I ever wrote, and, for good measure, told him that my paternal grandfather had been a rabbi from Poland. Then I explained my interest in bialystoker kuchen. "And, anyway," I concluded, "you're seeing me because Betty promised that you would."

Knowing he was licked, Leo Melamed finally asked me to sit down.

"The things I remember most about bialystoker kuchen

in Bialystok are feet," he began. "I was a little boy, only seven years old, when we fled from Bialystok in 1939, after the city was occupied first by the Germans and then by the Russians. Before that, my pretty young Aunt Bobble would take me to the kuchen bakery, holding my hand, and I stood on the floor and couldn't see over the grown-ups. All I saw were feet, but I loved the smell of the baking bread and the onions, and I was excited to be lifted up to watch the kuchen coming out of the oven. It was the essence of our meals. No matter what else was on the table, you could always use a kuchen."

Settling back in his chair, somewhat more relaxed, in the manner of a patient on a psychiatrist's couch, Leo Melamed warmed to the subject. "The bialy bakers were very innovative, and each one did a little something special—a little twist here, another twist there—to make his kuchen different. The bialy is really much better than the bagel, because without a hole, there is more surface to spread the butter or cream cheese. But if you want something really good, try one with schmaltz herring. My grandmother always gave me the tail piece, because I could use the tail as a handle and hold the piece upright and bite it without needing a fork."

The image of this trim, well-tailored tycoon, then sixty-three, biting into a chunk of herring that he held in one hand while clutching a bialy in the other is a sight I would have given a lot to see at that moment.

Besides recalling the nurturing scent of cholent baking in the oven from Friday afternoon to Saturday lunch ("When I say it was cooked, I really mean cooked . . ."), he described one of his most cherished food memories of his uncle who was a "pickle farmer." That meant that he grew cucumbers and pickled them with dill, garlic, salt, and spices and packed them in wooden barrels that were placed in a shallow lake to stay cool. The young Leo sometimes rowed out with his uncle to test the pickles. It was reassuring that this dyed-in-the-wool maven shares my view that new or half-sours (cucumbers held in brine only about ten days when made commercially) are not pickles at all but retain too much of the cucumber flavor, bright-green color, and hard skin; only bronze-green full-sours (in brine from two to four weeks) without any traces of the cucumber taste deserve the name. Along with an enduring love for the Yiddish language that he inherited from his father, Leo Melamed also inherited the love of salty foods. Let's hope that he also inherited low blood pressure.

The Hebrew word *melamed* means a teacher in an elementary Hebrew school (*cheder*), precisely the profession of Leo Melamed's parents, Isaac and Faygl Melamdovich. Leo said that they were staunch members of the Bund.

Known in Yiddish as *Algemeyner yidisher arbeter bund,* (United Jewish Workers Society), the Bund was begun by nonreligious, free-thinking intellectuals as a socialist labor movement, established in 1897 in Vilna in what is now Lithuania. The Bund sought to improve working and living conditions for the Jewish masses and to educate them, teaching and stressing Yiddish as a national language. (In the United States, Bund activities were continued by the Workman's Circle organization.)

The Melamdovich journey from Bialystok to the Midwest is chronicled in stunning detail in Leo Melamed's autobiography, *Back to the Futures,* published in 1996, a little over a year after our meeting. In it he describes a number of the events he told me about, including the escape that took the family through Vilna, Moscow, Siberia, and from Vladivostok to Yokohama. The Melamdovich family made that journey, as did about six thousand other Jews, with the help of Chiune Sugihara, the Japanese consul general in Vilna. Realizing what was about to happen, and without his government's approval, the heroic Sugihara issued Japanese transit visas to Jews for twenty-eight days, beginning on July 31, 1940. He did that only after securing travel permits from the Soviet government assuring their route to Vladivostok.

The family lived in Japan for about a year and finally got visas for America, landing in New York in April, 1941, just eight months before Pearl Harbor. The anxieties of that long trek left Leo Melamed with what he calls the Bialystok Syndrome: "Take care. Disaster lurks around the next corner." Not a bad motto for a commodities trader.

He was disappointed that he would have to move to Chicago when his parents obtained permanent teaching jobs in a Yiddish-language school. It's interesting to imagine the fate of the futures markets if he had stayed in New York instead of working as a runner on the floor of the Merc, a night job that enabled him to stay in John Marshall Law School by day.

Having first been impatient to get rid of me, and with the lights of Chicago coming on in the city below us, Leo Melamed so much enjoyed his subject that he even felt friendly toward me. He invited me on a tour of his warren of sleek offices, where computers clacked away nervously. Or maybe only I was nervous, feeling that with every click and clack, fortunes were being made—or lost—around the globe.

"Were bialys a basic food or a luxury when you were growing up in Bialystok?" I asked Max Ratner in my first telephone interview about a year after my return from Bialystok.

"Dahling! Food vas a luxury!" answered the eighty-five-year-old chairman of Forest City Enterprises, a vast publicly-traded construction company that grew out of a lumber business formed by Max, his four brothers, and a cousin in 1921. Now real estate developers, an assortment of second- and third-generation Ratners run the Forest City Commercial Group, with offices in various parts of the United States. The scrappy, generous Max Ratner and three brothers left Bialystok along with their mother, father, and four sisters in 1921. The bloody pogroms of 1905 (36 Jews killed) and 1906 (110 Jews killed) were warnings enough that they would all be better off in the *goldene medina* (the golden land that was America). "It's a good thing my brother Kalman—Charles—had gone over first and then came and got us," Ratner said.

"You know the Polacks [pejorative slang for Poles and much used by Jews] didn't need the Nazis to teach them anti-Semitism," Max Ratner said. "They got good at it all by themselves. I wouldn't give you two cents for most of them, although I know the Germans killed a lot of them too, and many Poles helped save Jews.

"In Bialystok, we lived in a house on the corner of Polna and Czysta streets, and there was a bialy bakery nearby. That bread was our main food. I remember my mother sending me for those kuchen before every *shabbes* and telling me not to buy any that were already made. I had to see them come right out of the oven. And we were not poor, but for Jews, life in Bialystok was not nice. Even if you did good business, you didn't always get paid on time. My father had forty workers in his clothing factory, and sometimes, to meet his Friday payroll, he had to borrow money from my uncle, who was a pharmacist. Those kuchen made up for a lot. All those onions and poppy seeds on the bagels made us feel good, even when we didn't have any butter to spread on them."

Ratner used the terms bagel and kuchen interchangeably, and he wasn't very patient with my questions about a hole versus an indented well. For once, I relented and let it ride. After that first conversation, I sent him a few dozen bialys from Kossar's, and his secretary called to say how much he liked them and that, after passing some around the office, he took the rest home.

Max Ratner soon sent me two extraordinary books as a thank-you gift. One was *The Bialystoker Memorial Book*— also known as the Yizkor (memorial) Book—for which he served on the editorial committee. It is a huge volume, with text in both English and Yiddish, devoted to memoirs from Bialystokers throughout the world, plus a history of the city and its commercial and social life and haunting old photographs throughout. In writing the foreword, Ratner told of the budding Zionism in Bialystok in the early 1880s, when the Russian-Polish BILU (the acronym for the Hebrew words meaning "House of Israel Go Forth") was formed. And in 1917, when the Balfour Declaration was signed, he remembered his mother donating her gold earrings to the cause of a Jewish homeland in Palestine.

The second book, *The Ratner House, 1888 to 1988*, is even more special. Put together by Max and Betty Ratner with professional help, it is an astounding and very handsome collection of family history and photographs— astounding because it's hard to imagine how so many old photographs remained safe for so long.

A few years later, after Max Ratner died, I called his son James, now the president of the corporation, to check some facts. He said that Max's older brother Charles had been a gambler and saved money to bring his family over. But before that, he had some trouble about his papers, and to avoid deportation, he joined the army of General John J. Pershing and served in the Philippines and the Panama Canal Zone, and during the Mexican Revolution, went in search of Pancho Villa. Somehow the thought of a new immigrant speaking Yiddish-accented English hunting for the great Mexican populist bandit seems the perfect plot for a typical Mel Brooks film. Too bad Wallace Beery isn't around to resurrect the role he made famous.

Jim Ratner told me that he did not hear much about bialys as a child, "because there simply were none in Cleveland to remind us." He added that occasionally his father brought some home from New York. "But what my father did talk about was that in Bialystok, it was very important to have a watermelon for Rosh Hashanah." (Try as I would, I found no mention of this custom, nor anyone who recalled it.)

Despite the absence of the kuchen, Jim Ratner thinks that Cleveland was the perfect place for his family to settle. "There were already more than a hundred thousand Jews living in the same neighborhood and my parents could walk through the streets and feel at home. There were five Yiddish newspapers and a very active Jewish social and cultural life. Also, Cleveland must have felt right. Bialystok was not a big city like Warsaw or Riga, and Cleveland was not a big city like New York or Chicago."

In his family book, Max recalls going to Sunday school every week and then to his grandparents' home, where they ate the hamburgers that they called by their Polish name, *kotleti* or cutlets. Jim Ratner expanded on the importance of family gatherings and food.

"Up until about fifteen years ago, all of the Ratners in Cleveland—and that's a lot of Ratners—gathered every Saturday night at one of our homes. And we always ate fried herring with potatoes boiled in their skins. They called the herring something that sounded like *pregeldi*."

Determined to track down the true form and meaning of that word, I searched through Polish dictionaries and cookbooks, as *pregeldi* suggested that language, but to no avail. I thought that perhaps Leo Melamed, being a Yiddishist, a Bialystoker, a herring lover, and a friend of the Ratners, might know the answer, but he had no clue.

Undoubtedly, the gods must have been watching over me, because once as I flipped through *Yiddish Cuisine*, a cookbook by Rabbi Robert Sternberg of St. Louis, I came across the recipe, *Gepregelte* Herring, described as being lightly fried. *Gepregelte* and pregeldi were close enough for me. I immediately faxed a flash to Leo Melamed, thinking I owed him an answer. He instantly faxed back, thanking me for the update and adding, "I did not need Jim Ratner to tell me about *gepregelte* which, of course, does mean lightly fried—and sometimes not so lightly."

Bialystokers apparently thought that the flavor of herring was well suited to kuchen. "What I loved best was to dip a piece of kuchen into the salt brine from schmaltz herring," said Sam Solasz, the former president of the Bialystok Center in New York. "We did that whenever we could, back in Bialystok." Now a successful wholesale meat dealer, Solasz was born just outside of Bialystok and lived in that city until he was fourteen. After that, he went through a series of escapes from the Nazis, served in the Russian army, spent time in displaced-persons camps in Germany, then went to Israel, and finally came to the United States in 1951. He returns to Bialystok every August for the memorial service for the sixty thousand Jews who were killed there. "I don't go back because I love the Poles," he told me. "I go back so they will never forget!"

There were two other delightful and valuable respondents of bialy memoirs, both of whom I interviewed by telephone but was not fortunate enough to meet.

About eight months after my 1992 trip to Poland, I received a note on flowered paper, written in a pretty cursive handwriting. It came from Hannah Sielecka in Queens. She introduced herself as an old friend of Dr. Anatol Leszczyn- ski, who had been so helpful in Warsaw. He wanted to report that Janosz, our driver, was going to Lublin to look for the kuchen baker and perhaps would bring back good information. When I called to thank Mrs. Sielecka, she instantly volunteered:

"So my sveetie, ask me anything. I am happy to tell you," she said in a cozy voice. "You know, I am really from Bia- lystok. Many people say they are but are not. We used to buy kuchen on Urovetska Street. I liked the crisp center, and my brother liked the soft rim, so we would break the kuchen and share. We used to have our big meal at two in the afternoon, and we ate kuchen with everything because they are pareve [neutral foods that laws of kashrut permit with either meat or dairy products]. I have tried them here many times, but they never taste right. We ate pletzls too, but they were different.

"I remember many breads that I loved as a child, and though some of them here look the same, they do not taste or smell the same. We had kaiser rolls, and sweet yeast breads called in Polish placki that was like coffee cake, and przekladance, which was filled with raisins, prunes, cheese, or nuts. We ate those with coffee. Then there was black bread, and on Friday and Saturday, we had challah. On Saturday night, my mother always gave us herring and potatoes, and every day a different soup."

Two weeks later, she called again, "Sveetie, I have news, but not good. Janosz says there are no kuchen in Lublin."

Hannah Sielecka lived alone but had a son somewhere in South America, who visited her occasionally and wanted her to move down there to be near him. "But I have traveled so much, and I am too tired for a new place," she said.

After hearing of the ordeals she endured between Bialystok and New York, I could understand why she wanted to stay put. She told me about her father's being taken to a concentration camp in 1940 with her brother, never to be seen again, and how she stayed behind with her mother, who was too sick to be moved.

I gradually pieced together bits of her strange jigsaw-puzzle story. When she and her mother went to Lithuania, where they expected to meet her father, she carried a small cache of family jewelry. The Russian NKVD arrested them and wanted to send them to a work camp, but weirdly observing some sort of Kafkaesque law, they needed a signed confession from Hannah, admitting that she was an enemy smuggling jewels out of Russia. She refused, telling them that the Germans were the enemies they should kill, not her and her mother.

"When you are young, you are not afraid, so you do not think of consequences," Hannah said of her refusal to sign. Then followed a series of tortures to get her to comply, the most horrific being that she was tied to a sled while in thin nightclothes and put out in the freezing snow overnight. Then they took her to a basement, where a single bright light bulb hung and a slow drip of water kept tapping on her head. She refused to sign, even on the threat of hanging. Her interrogator, who, she remembered, smoked a pipe with a devil's-head bowl that had glinting green glass eyes, finally said that if she signed, she could have anything she wanted.

"I told them, 'First you give me my wish and then I will sign,'" Hannah said.

"And what is your wish?" the man asked.

"To go to New York City, America," she answered.

This enraged him so much that he reached into a drawer for what she thought was a gun to kill her with, but instead, he pushed a button that called a guard. "Take her away!" he ordered, and she went back to the room where her mother was nervously waiting.

"I was so proud of not signing, and I never regretted it," she said.

After her mother died of an illness, Hannah and a friend escaped and found work in a Russian seaport she did not name. "They had no one to do hard work. All the men were in the army or dead. So they didn't ask questions about who you were or where you came from. I was then seventeen or eighteen, and we were given the job of loading huge, heavy bags of salt onto ships by climbing rope ladders. The wind was terrible, and the ladders swayed and bags of salt fell into the sea. I hated that job and soon went to work repairing railroad tracks."

Surviving in Stalingrad during the monumental German siege, she finally was free at the war's end. In 1944 or 1945 she somehow got to the United States. I asked her if the events she lived through seemed real.

"I sometimes ask myself," she said. " 'Did that really happen or did I see it in a movie?' "

My last news from Hannah Sielecka was that Dr. Anatol Leszczynski had died, and then I lost track of her. I like to think that she is with her son, happily settled in sunny Brazil or Argentina.

• • •

After being interviewed about my trip to Bialystok by Joan Hamburg, the longtime host of one of New York's most popular daytime radio talk shows, one of her friends, who was listening, put me in touch with Barbara Levin. The wife of Senator Carl Levin of Michigan, Barbara is the daughter of Ben Halpern, the ex-Bialystoker who was 101 years old when he died in September 1999.

"I'll give you his number, and I'll tell him to expect your call," Barbara generously said. "He'll be so happy to talk to you. His mind is as sharp as ever."

"You live in New York?" Ben Halpern began. "I envy you. Such a rich culture, so many wonderful things to do. In Bialystok, I lived on the same street as Zamenhof, the Esperanto man, and we knew the Litvinov family very well. Only their name was Wallach.

"I lived there until I was about twenty, and kuchen were our main meat, morning, noon, and night. We loved to have them with smoked fish for *vechere* [Polish for evening, but Yiddish for supper]. I also ate them with halvah, and I alternated bites between the halvah and the kuchen. When I went every day to cheder, my mother always gave me a buttered kuchen to eat on the way," Ben Halpern said. "I held it in my hand, of course, and one day a streetwalker came along and she begged for money, which I did not have to give her. So she grabbed my kuchen and ran away eating it. I still remember how hungry I was in school that day. Bialys in Detroit don't taste like the real ones, so I'm still hungry.

"But tell me, you say you are writing a book about kuchen? How many words can you say about them?"

When I answered, "About thirty thousand," Ben Halpern said, "Really! Then maybe you'll have a few left over to say something about spachky."

I could find no trace of such a food in any Yiddish cookbook, nor did his daughter know what he meant. My guess is that Mr. Halpern was remembering *pąsczki*, the small Polish yeast doughnuts that are filled with thick jam and sprinkled with confectioners' sugar. Having enjoyed *pąsczki* at A. Blikle, the Warsaw bakery that is famous for them, I could certainly muster up about five thousand words on their behalf, if not thirty thousand.

"I was born in Zabludov, about sixteen miles from Bialystok," Ben Halpern told me during one of our three telephone conversations. "But I lived in Bialystok before, during, and after the First World War. My parents could hardly feed themselves, so I worked and also went to school and learned to be a bookkeeper. It was hard to get work, because Bialystok was cut off from Germany, and there was nowhere else for the textile mills to sell fabric. I had a rich uncle who said to me one day, 'Pesach [Passover] is coming, and there are no matzohs in Bialystok. Take this money and go to

Odessa and bring a hundred pounds back. We will make a lot of money.'

"While I was in Odessa, the Germans took over Bialystok, and there was no way for me to get back. But they were short of matzohs in Odessa, too, so the baker was happy to take them back. He returned most of my money. I only lost a few rubles."

Describing a complicated series of jobs, Ben Halpern said that like the Germans and the Russians, the Poles were also dangerous enemies "Russian anti-Semitism was with the masses and against capitalists. The Polacks let the Jews work and make money, but they stole the money and beat us up, and if a Jewish man with a beard walked by, Polish roughnecks would grab him and pull out the hairs of his beard, one by one.

"My parents figured out that my brother, Max, would not be able to get work, so they sent him to America in 1913, and shortly after the war I followed him to Detroit. I couldn't find a job, because in those days all the bookkeeping was done by women, so I joined my brother in the little fish store he had established."

Eventually Ben Halpern opened and prospered with a fish market in Ypsilanti, where he was able to ride out the Depression, but not before he had also delved into the sausage casing business with an uncle in Chile. Figuring that they could make a killing if they could find enough casings to supply the American market when the Second World War made such products scarce, he went to Chile to develop a source. Air travel was slow and difficult during wartime, with many stops en route, and it took him eight days to get there and eight more to get back.

"I was afraid that I looked suspicious to one customs officer, because he kept staring at me when I stopped in Kingston, Jamaica. He took me into a room and closed the door and asked me what I was doing and where I had stopped along the way. He then asked me where I was born. I answered Zabludov. I was surprised that he wrote it down correctly without asking me how to spell it. I asked him how he knew that name.

" 'Because I am from Bielsk,' he said, naming a nearby town in the Bialystok province. 'How is your brother Max?' "

S E V E N

———›»●‹‹———

F R O M   B I A L Y S T O K   T O   P A R I S

"What are you doing on the rue des Rosiers on such a freezing cold Sunday morning?" Elie Wiesel asked as we met in
Bibliophane, a Jewish bookstore where he was signing
copies of his new book.

"Looking for bialys," I answered.

"In Paris? Good luck!"

My search through the Marais district on that icy Sunday in
November, 1998, was not the first I had made there, trying
to find someone who remembered Bialystoker kuchen. But
as I was in Paris to do a story on bistros for the *New York
Times*, I thought one more try wouldn't hurt. Besides, it

would have been rare indeed for me to spend even a few days in that city without going to the colorful and familiar eight-hundred-year-old Jewish quarter. Dick and I loved to walk along the narrow, winding rue des Rosiers, always fascinated by Jews speaking French-accented Yiddish and Yiddish-accented French, eating lox and bagels and salami omelets with pickles amid the Hebrew signs announcing kosher butchers, bakeries, appetizer stores, restaurants, and shops offering Judaica, diamonds, and furs at discount prices. Like the Lower East Side of New York, the Marais is especially convivial on a Sunday morning, when all businesses come to life after having been closed for the Saturday Sabbath. We also turned the corner to rue Pavée to take yet another look at the lyrical art nouveau facade of the Agoudas Hakehilos synagogue, designed in 1913 by Hector Guimard, the architect whose wife was Jewish and who is most famous for his cast-iron decorations for the Metro.

I never walk through the Marais without recalling my first visit to Paris, in 1953, when there was a black market in French francs. Guided by a Parisian friend, I went to a money changer who had a tiny, barren grocery store on this same rue des Rosiers. I gave him dollars, and he went to a small back room and reached into a refrigerator, then handed me a stack of chilled franc notes that gave new meaning to the term "cold cash."

One Sunday, after such a transaction, I went into the popular kosher-style delicatessen, Goldenberg's, for lunch and stopped to ogle the cold appetizer buffet. Suddenly, I had a gefilte fish epiphany. For alongside that label were not the oval dumplings of poached fish I knew, but instead, a whole, long, slim fish, something like a pike, plumply stuffed (*gefilte*) complete with head, tail, and skin intact, all shiny under a faintly golden aspic inset with rounds of carrots and halved black olives. It was served in two refined slices filled with the familiar ground fish and onion forcemeat, garnished with dicings of the white wine aspic, surely the most elegant version of that dish that I have ever seen. "Leave it to the French," I thought. "Even when they cook Jewish." This was, in fact, the first experience that made me curious about how differently traditional ethnic dishes might be interpreted from one country to another and, in a way, ultimately lead to my search for international bialy variations.

Forty-six years later, I was going back to Goldenberg's, as well as to the two Finkelsztajn bakeries, wondering what spin the French might put on the bialystoker kuchen. Again, no one had heard of them, but all surely knew pletzls. But alas, in the three places, pletzls were big, shiny, puffy rounds of bread that must have been made with eggs, so that the spongy texture was closer to challah than to pletzl or kuchen. They were, in fact, very much like the misbegotten kuchen produced by the gentile baker in Bialystok. Finkelsztajn's pletzls were less sweet than Goldenberg's, and had a little more *geshmak,* or flavor, but were too soft and sissified to be worthy of their name.

If I would not have luck with bialys, I expected to be more fortunate with my other research in Paris that November. After many failed attempts, I at last was to meet two of my earliest correspondents in person. One was Dr. Samuel Pisar, the internationally famous lawyer, who was born in Bialystok and was one of the youngest survivors of Auschwitz. The other was Charles "Shleimeh" Zabuski whom I contacted after reading an article he wrote for the *Bialystoker Shtimme* and who had responded with helpful suggestions.

Samuel Pisar's name had been suggested to me more than any other, most especially by the late Izaak Rybal and by Tomasz Wisniewski in Bialystok. In addition to his legal and diplomatic work, Pisar's best-selling autobiography, *Of Blood and Hope*, published in 1979, recounted his growing up in a prominent, well-to-do Bialystok family, his experiences with Soviets and Nazis, his wanderings to find a place in the world in England, Australia, the United States, and France, his clients that have included Elizabeth Taylor, Ava

Gardner, the International Olympics Committee, and the late British magnate Sir James Goldsmith, who was his close friend. He was an adviser to Presidents Kennedy and Nixon, Nelson Rockefeller, and Golda Meir, among others, and he accompanied Giscard d'Estaing to a memorial service at Auschwitz and Henry Kissinger to Mexico City.

Impressed, in 1993 I wrote a most careful letter to Samuel Pisar at his New York office and described my quest. His secretary said that he spent most of his time in his Paris office, but when he next returned to New York, she would give him my letter. She had no idea when that might be, and her voice made me feel I would have to wait a very long time. To my surprise, I had a phone call from Pisar himself, not more than five days later.

"Because *Of Blood and Hope* has been translated into twenty languages," he began, "I am constantly asked for interviews on matters such as the Holocaust, international economics and law, politics and social policies, and I try to avoid such appointments. But in all of those years, you are the first to ask about bialystoker kuchen, and so I could not resist your request."

He then told me much of the following and called back two days later to say that he couldn't stop thinking about bialys and wanted to tell me more.

"Bialys were invented in Bialystok and were made by

Jewish bakers and they were prevalent, a staple of our diet. They always had onions and poppy seeds and were better than those we get in New York. They had very crisp centers, and it was very important to hear the crackle and feel the snap when you broke one. The rims were very soft and squashy and the center was thinner than those we get here. Sometimes a kuchen would come out of the oven burned on top and soggy in the center. I hated that."

Samuel Pisar said that they never ate smoked salmon or any other fish with bialys, something he considers an Americanization.

"I can feel and smell them now as I talk to you and I search for them with a passion everywhere I go. It's not the taste so much as the symbol. It reminds me of coming home safely from school in the late afternoons of Bialystok's long, dark season. I can still hear the women vendors carrying hot kuchen in big straw baskets as they went through the streets yelling at the top of their lungs, 'Kuchen, kuchen, heisse kuchen. . . .' They had to be heiss, not cold. My grandmother, who lived with us, would spread butter or cream cheese on the back of a kuchen without cutting it open, and I would munch it as I went out to play with friends."

Because I wanted to meet as many of my respondents as possible, and especially the very eloquent Pisar, I tried several times, but nothing seemed convenient until this visit to

Paris. And so one Saturday morning, I shuffled through autumn leaves on the quiet, parklike avenue Foch, following instructions to ring a bell that would open a big iron gate that would lead me to the private courtyard rimmed with elegant houses, some of which were foreign embassies. One had been the home of the late brilliant pianist Artur Rubinstein, who was a friend of Samuel Pisar and his wife, Judith.

From glimpses of their foyer, living room, and dining room as I entered, it was obvious that the Pisars share a taste for impeccable European modern furniture, as well as paintings and sculptures, many of which, I learned, had been gifts from the artists themselves or from grateful clients. As we began to talk in his richly cluttered book-lined study, with its mellow wood paneling, the trim Pisar, then sixty-nine, smartly casual in a checked sport jacket and pale yellow shirt, served me coffee and a small pastry he called a Mikado. It was a gold-foil-wrapped slim long rectangle of layered gaufrette wafers iced with chocolate, much like an upper-class chocolate-covered Nabisco wafer.

Although he loved that pastry, he said, he had to apologize for its not being a bialy, which he rates with the very best foods in the world. "I can get pretty good ones when I am in my homes in New York or Florida," he said. "But in Paris I have to make do with things such as caviar, foie gras, and croissants. I know that the bagel is in full flower now, and many prefer it because it is softer and they like the hole, but I feel such people are heretics.

"When my book was published in Polish, I was invited back to Bialystok to be honored by the mayor of the town. I spoke in a big hall that was full, and I asked if there was anyone in the audience who remembered kuchen, which I described in detail. No one raised a hand, but as we were breaking up, an old, bent woman came up and said she remembered the kind of bread I described but did not think any was being baked. She was not born in Bialystok but had settled there after the war, when she came out of hiding in the woods."

Noting that in addition to English, he speaks Polish, Russian, Yiddish, Hebrew, French, German, and more, Pisar said, "Auschwitz was a great Berlitz." He described how his mother saved him from a death camp when, after abandoning their beautiful home and being locked into the Bialystok ghetto, they were finally rounded up for deportation to concentration camps. Although he recently had had his bar mitzvah in a shabby synagogue just inside the barbed-wire fence of the ghetto, he was considered too young for long pants. But his mother, relying on her maternal sixth sense, had him wear them because he would then look old enough to be a laborer and so was spared for a work camp.

As he was marched off to a cattle train of the sort that

eventually would take him to concentration camps such as Maidanek, Auschwitz, and Dachau, he looked back for what would be his last glimpse of his mother and his sister. "I was in Auschwitz from the age of thirteen to fifteen," he said, "and it was there that they tattooed this number on my arm. I think, because I was young and still flexible, I recovered from the nightmare better than many older men." From their photographs in Pisar's book, his mother, Helen, and his father, David, were extraordinarily handsome. As with so many of the photographs of Bialystokers I saw in the various memorial books, they had dark, reproachful eyes that seem to burn through the page, like those on faces in the glowing, haunting coffin paintings done in encaustics in western Egypt during the Roman period, most especially around the town of Fayum.

Understandably, Samuel Pisar is unrelenting and famously outspoken on the subject of anti-Semitism and the aftermaths of the Holocaust, for which he uses the Hebrew word, Shoah. In October, 1998, when he presented the Nostra Aetate Award of the Center for Christian-Jewish Understanding to Cardinal Jean-Marie Lustiger, the cardinal of Paris who was born Jewish, he leavened the more usual words of praise with a few typically Pisarian zingers.

Speaking at the Sutton Place Synagogue in New York, in front of dignitaries who included the late John Cardinal O'Connor of New York and René-Samuel Sirat, the chief rabbi of Paris, Pisar said that when he was an adolescent in Auschwitz, he felt that if Jesus, his mother Mary, and the twelve apostles had been alive in his time, they would surely all have been in Auschwitz, because their blood was as tainted as his.

"By placing the sins of the world on Jewish shoulders," Pisar said, "noted Christian thinkers and inquisitors have at times turned their backs on Christ himself, opening the way to persecution and mayhem."

He praised Cardinal Lustiger's successful efforts to relocate the crosses that the Catholic church erected at Auschwitz. Then, as a closing, this man, who had convinced Leonard Bernstein that it would be inappropriate to compose an opera based on the Holocaust, made another special plea. He asked that the recently canonized Sister Teresa Benedicta, the converted Jew born Edith Stein, be commemorated on the day of the traditional Shoah observance instead of on the date of her death, because she was gassed at Auschwitz, not as a Carmelite nun, but as a Jew.

"Halvah you don't eat mit kuchen! Halvah you eat mit brot!" Charles "Shleimeh" Zabuski informed me emphatically in a mix of Yiddish and English when we met in Paris a few days later. I was delighted at last to meet him and overlooked his obvious exasperation as though talking to a child who just wasn't getting it.

At seventy-seven, and after having survived all of the worst horrors of the Holocaust save only death, this still ruggedly handsome Bialystoker with silky white hair could easily pass for a prosperous New York cloak-and-suiter, the kind of high roller I could imagine wearing a camel's-hair sports coat at a racetrack. Shleimeh Zabuski's hazel eyes misted as he reminisced, "Butter was expensive, but when we could, we spread it on top, over the poppy seeds and onion. Otherwise, we ate the bagelech plain." (Along with Max Ratner, Shleimeh—also called "Shlomo" and "Shlermeh"—used the terms bagel and kuchen interchangeably.)

Like so many of the Bialystokers I met, Shleimeh Zabuski had written a book, and he thoughtfully brought a copy for me. *Needle and Thread: A Tale of Survival from Bialystok to Paris* was actually written and published by his American cousin, June Sutz Brott, a teacher, editor, and writer whom he visited several times in Oakland, California. As he told his story in French and Yiddish, Mrs. Brott, with the help of friends who translated, put the whole thing down in graceful English, often, Shleimeh said, with tear-filled eyes. Although the only way to do the incredible story justice would be to completely reprint it here, a few highlights that were described to me by Zabuski at least hint of the epic whole.

As the title of his book indicates, Zabuski was a tailor, a trade he learned reluctantly from his father in Bialystok but one that saw him through the worst times in labor camps such as Blizhin because his skill was useful to the Germans. It later gave him a livelihood in Paris, until he retired in 1985.

Shleimeh Zabuski decided not to go to the United States from Paris, even though he found surviving relatives in Chicago who would sponsor him. By that time, he and his second wife, Adela, a survivor he met in Germany after liberation, were exhausted from traveling and had already settled in Paris and were learning French and working at steady jobs. "It was the biggest mistake of our lives," Shleimeh told me, "because in America, I would have been with some family." They had chosen Paris, he said, because he could not find any relatives and Adela's brother Jacques had been a leader in the French resistance and Communist movements and had many contacts who could help them get established.

He was in a way repeating the family history. His father, Mordecai Zabuski, realized his dream of moving to Argentina in 1919, after the bloody pogroms of 1905 and 1906 convinced him that Jews could not have a good future in what was then Russia. He reluctantly returned to Bialystok to marry his fiancée, Sarah Sutz, who was afraid to follow him to Buenos Aires as she had originally agreed to do. It was clearly the biggest mistake of their lives, as both died in concentration camps, along with twelve of their fif-teen family members. Survivors included Shleimeh's uncle, Ben Sutz, who had been sent to America by his parents after the pogrom of 1906. Shleimeh also lost his first wife and two infant sons through illness and starvation. He regards his one son, Michael, fifty-one, whose mother was Adela, as a cherished blessing. After Adela died in 1985, Shleimeh married his present wife, Simone Fremont.

Shleimeh's relatives in America quickly sent him a Singer sewing machine and money. He has visited them several times, including his uncle Ben, Sarah Sutz Brott's father, who died at 102 after years in Sun City, Arizona. Years ago, when Zabuski stopped in New York en route to his family in the West, he visited Izaak Rybal at the Bia-lystoker Center and Home for the Aged, so that he could speak with some of the elderly Bialystok émigrés who were still there. He also reported that the kuchen he had in New York were good, but not like those in Bialystok.

What stands out throughout the Zabuski biography is the constant search for food. Living among poor Jewish neighbors in his childhood, he recalls an evening when his mother had just finished frying latkes—potato pancakes—in her iron skillet. Just then a neighbor's little girl came and asked if her mother could borrow the skillet, because she didn't have one. When Sarah Zabuski said that she would first wash it, the child asked her not to. Her mother had just enough money for potatoes, she said, but none for oil, so the greasy pan would be fine.

Things were even more serious in the camps, where getting enough food to stay alive, both for Shleimeh and his father, took up most of their time. Like Pisar, Zabuski said that he dreamed of kuchen and especially of their aroma. He and his father quickly learned the trick of going to the camp wall at night and throwing over some extra piece of clothing that they had, for which the guards would throw back bread, a boiled potato, or, with luck, a bit of kielbasa sausage. Chapters with titles such as "Sunflower Seeds, Potato Pancakes, the Apple, Two Turnips" and "Bread" tell of food strife and strategies in infamous labor camps such as Maidanek, Blizhin, Lehren-Lagen, Auschwitz-Birkenau, and Flossenburg.

When I asked Shleimeh Zabuski if he believes in God after all of the suffering of the Holocaust, he said he did not, especially since he observed that those treated the worst by the Germans were the most religious who wore beards, *peyes* (earlocks), and the ritual skullcaps known as yarmulkes or *kippot*.

———⟫●⟪———

EIGHT

BIALYS IN THE
PROMISED LAND

"Forget the milk and honey. Just take me to your bialys," I imagined myself saying as Dick and I embarked on our first trip to Israel in 1994, just two years after we had visited Bialystok. My assignment was to write about food and restaurants in Tel Aviv and Jerusalem for the *Condé Nast Traveler*, but as usual, my secret mission was to pursue my research on the bialy.

In Israel, that meant finally meeting Yerachmiel Giladi, Arieh Shamir, and Lipa Avinadov. As a result of my article in the *Bialystoker Shtimme*, I had been corresponding with and speaking to Giladi and Shamir for a year and a half before this visit. Both assured me that they had many

———⟫●⟪———

memories of kuchen in Bialystok, but they knew of no retail bakery in Israel that made them. Both also wrote of Lipa Avinadov, a fellow émigré who always brought kuchen to gatherings of Bialystokers. That name was rapidly becoming familiar to me, for it was also mentioned by a Bialystoker correspondent in Australia who had attended such a meeting in Israel.

Unfortunately, no one had any idea where Lipa got the kuchen because his source was a closely guarded secret.

Certain that Lipa was a missing link to kuchen culture, I wanted to arrange to see him in Israel before I left New York. Typical of the elusiveness of information that had dogged me throughout my research on the bialy, no one seemed to know Lipa's telephone number, and neither Giladi nor Shamir knew in which town he lived, only that it was neither Tel Aviv nor Jerusalem. But all referred me to Michael Fliker, who is the head of the Bialystoker *landsleit* in Israel and of Kiryat Bialystok, the neighborhood for Bialystokers in Yehud, a town outside of Tel Aviv. After two phone calls, I realized that getting information from the reluctant, taciturn Fliker would not be easy, probably because he was suspicious of any stranger asking for a friend's address, especially a woman calling from New York. Figuring that it would take badgering by one of the world's most delightful and craftiest badgerers, I telephoned Sussi Pundik, a Danish Jew and a valued friend who lives in Tel Aviv. Also of Ashkenazi background, as I am, Sussi insisted, as had many others, that what I called a bialy or a kuchen was a pletzl, pure and simple.

"My mother-in-law from Germany used to bake exactly what you describe—but bigger—and she called it a pletzl," Sussi insisted, no matter how many times I described the indented well as being critical to the Bialystoker kuchen. But she went all out to help me—first because she is exquisitely generous, but also because she is used to dealing with obsessive journalists, as her husband, Herbert, was for many years the editor-in-chief of *Politiken*, the leading liberal newspaper in Denmark, to which he still contributes articles on Asia and the Middle East.

Finally, Sussi, who speaks Hebrew, wrested from Fliker the telephone number of Lipa Avinadov. It turned out that he lived in the small town of Gedera, about 25 miles southeast of Tel Aviv. When I called him from New York, he proved to be most friendly and forthcoming, explaining that he was born in 1923 and that he had a very successful construction company, in which his children and their spouses worked. He was also proud of being the only source of authentic Bialystoker kuchen in Israel or, as he put it, "maybe even in the world." Lipa was delighted at the prospect of my visiting Gedera, and he promised to take me to Mordecai Zananni, a baker who would demonstrate his kuchen procedures. "I have tried kuchen in New York four or five times, but they are very pale," Lipa said in parting. "They don't look like my kuchelach and they don't taste like my kuchelach."

On a bright and sunny morning, Dick and I set out with a driver for Gedera. Riding along the luminous Mediterranean coast and then turning inland to roads lined with eucalyptus trees and fruit orchards, we explained to Ehud, our driver, what our quest was all about. A little less than an hour later, as we pulled into the parking lot of Lipa's construction company, Ehud asked if he could have a kuchen to taste. Since converts were needed to bring bialy fervor to Israel, we promised to give him enough to take home to his wife and two children.

Lipa, our short, stocky, muscular host, then seventy-one, was waiting outside to greet us with crushingly firm handshakes. Casually but immaculately dressed in the favored costume of Israeli men—light-colored pants and a tieless, short-sleeved sport shirt—Lipa took us into the office and introduced his daughter, Malka, who assured me that she loves kuchen, "except when I am on a diet."

After meeting several other family members, we drove to the little town that turned out to be charming, sylvan, and slightly hilly, much like villages in the Hudson River Valley of upstate New York. Lipa explained that Gedera was settled by the first Zionists, the BILU immigrants from Russia in 1884, and a few of their picturesque little wooden houses in the oldest part of the town still survive, all painted a dark, borscht-red and many with decorative jigsaw carving trim and lush, pocket-size gardens overflowing with red and purple hibiscus. In the Museum for the History of Gedera and the Biluim, neatly laid out in a formal turn-of-the-century house, we followed the story of the BILU migration to Israel and the travails of the early settlers (students, including thirteen boys and one girl). Their struggles and gradual progress is told through photographs and documents. Fighting adverse conditions, such as brackish water and hostile neighbors, and provided only with one gun, one dog, and eight pickaxes, they established a settlement, later to be joined by Jews from Yemen, Poland, and between 1933 and 1939, from Germany.

As we walked along the quiet streets shortly before noon, a loud, wailing alarm sounded. Lipa explained that it was an alert signal in case of an Arab attack and that it was tested daily at this time. We soon learned that our gruff but friendly host was a loyal member of the Likud Party.

The bakery was in a house that indicated just how successful Mordecai Zananni had become. It was a vast, wide sort of manor-chalet, with three floors occupied by the baker, his wife, and four children. The bakery was below, in a basement, and the oven spanning the entire width was a low tunnellike construction, fired by gas and stone-lined. Bending down and looking through the blazing yellow waves of heat, I thought it seemed like an eternity of hell— or heaven, if full of kuchen.

Bialystoker kuchen going into the oven at Mordecai Zananni's bakery. Gedera, Israel, 1999. *Photograph by Giora Raz.*

The room smelled even better than Kossar's, what with the onions and yeast and the added zest of toasting poppy seeds. The small, swarthy baker, Mordecai Zananni, and the workers that sometimes included his children, mixed dough, kneaded it, shaped mounds and then balls, and with their fingers, pressed in the critical center well. Then each round was brushed with water and sprinkled liberally with poppy seeds and chopped fresh onions. As far as I could tell, the biggest difference between those bialys and their New York counterparts was the flour. Zananni's seemed to have more gluten and was browner and grainier even than our own whole-wheat flour. The bread was also saltier and emerged from the oven crackling crisp in just seven minutes.

It was truly a wonderful, toasty, chewy bialy, but the grainy flour made it more filling than the New York variety. Having trained my palate on my hometown bialys, I am afraid that, despite the absence of poppy seeds, Kossar's still set the standard for me, familiarity being the seasoning that counts. Calvin Trillin once wrote that any man who doesn't think his hometown hamburger is the best is a sissy. That may be true of bialys as well.

Lipa had ordered a big batch of kuchen for us, and we went to his tidy, bright home to have some, then fresh from the oven. His housekeeper made coffee, because, he explained sadly, his wife had died about a year earlier. We sat on a comfortable screened porch as Lipa told us that he had gone back to Bialystok four times looking for traces of his childhood, sometimes with his son and Tomasz Wisniewski as a guide, and each time he returned to Israel more depressed by memories.

As we ate buttered warm bialys with good strong coffee, Lipa recalled how he came to develop these kuchen, after years of longing for their homey flavor. "When I first tasted Mordecai's pita in Gedera, something seemed very familiar about them. I took a few to a friend, also from Bialystok, and I said, 'You know, Moishe, this pita has a special *geschmack* and with a few touches, these could be perfect kuchelach,' and Moishe agreed."

Lipa then instructed the baker on the size, shape, and indentation and on the topping of poppy seeds and onions; the rest is bialy history. Unfortunately for everyone else in Israel, Mr. Zananni still restricts himself to pita, with which he is so successful that trucks line up at his bakery every morning, for deliveries to Tel Aviv and beyond. He makes bialys only for Lipa Avinadov, in large quantities on special order. Just before our visit, Lipa had ordered five hundred kuchen for the *bris* (ritual circumcision ceremony) of a new grandson.

"Zananni's kuchen are ninety-five percent like those I bought for my mother in Bialystok when I was a child," Lipa continued. "There was a bakery every hundred and fifty meters, but only in the Jewish section. The goyim couldn't afford them. I loved them with butter, cheese, and halvah that we got from a store called The Macedonian. But I also ate them with pastrami—delicious! Our favorite baker was Moishe Mendl at Number Twelve Gieldova Street," said Lipa, mentioning the same baker my two Australian correspondents named.

The youngest of three children, Lipa was the only one in his family to survive the Holocaust after being in eight concentration camps, among them Mauthausen in Austria and, in Poland, Treblinka, Maidanek, and Auschwitz. He went to Israel in 1945 and settled in Gedera, where he eventually went into construction work, although his father's business had been textiles.

"When I was only twelve, I worked with my father and knew every customer," Lipa recalled. "He specialized in a fabric known as Bialystok *tuch*, a very fine wool used for coats."

Lipa's family name in Poland was Lozanski but, like so many other Jews who went to Israel, he changed the European name to Avinadov, which is of Hebrew origin. As Sussi Pundik explained, many second- and third-generation Israelis, in search of roots, were switching back to the European names their families had for centuries.

We left finally with hugs instead of handshakes, and we took along about five dozen kuchen, thereby filling the car with the yeasty aroma of hot baked bread and roasted onions. Ehud grabbed a bialy from the dozen we gave him and began eating. When he finished, he reached for another, saying, "When you taste one, you want another," surely an advertising slogan in the making. Our proselytizing seemed to have worked, and he was hooked, but we doubted that any kuchen would make it to his family. We then dropped another dozen at Sussi Pundik's pretty house on Hazait Street in the old residential section of Tel Aviv where streets are named for the trees, *hazait* meaning olive.

Sussi looked into the bag, pulled out a kuchen, and announced triumphantly, "See? Pletzl!"

When we got back to the Tel Aviv Hilton, I gave another dozen kuchen to Guy Klaiman, then the food and beverage manager of that hotel. He cut each in half and placed twenty-four freshly warmed pieces on the breakfast buffet the next morning, reporting that they went like, well, hot kuchen.

The next morning I packed some more kuchen, and with Sussi driving, we went to meet Yerachmiel Giladi. He lived in Kfar Saba, a town about 45 minutes north of Tel Aviv, an area that had been mostly orange groves. I told Sussi what I knew about Giladi from his three gentle, informative letters, all painstakingly written in Hebrew script that looked as though birds had dipped their little toenails in blue ink, then skittered across the page.

Translated, the first letter began, "I read your article about bialys in the *Shtimme* and found it very interesting. The Sheraton name is world famous because of the hotels. Are they yours? [No.] I don't know how the kuchen look or taste in New York, but as one who ate them every day in Bialystok, I cannot forget how they tasted there, even though I left in 1929. It was not for nothing that the Yidden [Jews] from the city were called Bialystoker kuchen fressers.

"Once, when we had a meeting of Israeli Bialystokers on a Saturday evening, the artist Moishe Becker asked, 'How come you are eating kuchen and tea on Saturday night when for that meal Jews in Bialystok always ate herring and potatoes that were boiled in their skins?'"

Giladi wrote that what they ate on Saturday night was raw salt herring with no smetena—sour cream—and that the skins were peeled off as the potatoes were eaten. But that reference to herring and unpeeled boiled potatoes reiterated what Jim Ratner of Cleveland recalled, although his family's herring was *gepregelte*—fried.

Giladi also wrote about Dr. Ludwik Zamenhof, who died in 1917 after inventing Esperanto, which Giladi learned to speak in 1928. When he was able to retire from his construction business, Giladi attended Esperantist conferences in Portland, Oregon and Vancouver, London, Cuba, and China. "I am eighty-five, but Esperanto keeps the human being young and conscientious for a long time. About five hundred of us meet once a month in Tel Aviv and speak only that language. There are streets named after Zamenhof in several Israeli cities. My wife thinks all Esperantists are meshugge [crazy]," he said. Indeed, a few years later, when my friend Dalia Carmel, an Israeli living in New York, called Yerachmiel Giladi to check on some of the information for this book, his wife answered, saying, "If you don't speak Esperanto, he won't talk to you!"

As we approached Kfar Saba, we saw patches of orange trees, more like garden ornaments than like a serious crop.

Yerachmiel Giladi turned out to be slightly built, with fair hair and bright blue eyes, shy and energetic despite some heart problems. He apologized because his wife was recovering from an illness and so could not greet us. We walked around his garden, picked a few oranges, and then went inside the modestly proportioned wood-paneled cottage, typical of those built for early settlers in the 1930s.

Giladi carefully put the bialys in his freezer, calling them "kukoj," the plural in Esperanto, and he said that the scent reminded him of early morning in the small store where his mother sold kuchen to supplement the income of his father, who was a tailor. He also described the differences and similarities between Arabic pita and kuchen, which he translated as "pie-cake."

"We ate the pie-cake with butter that we spread in the center well and around the soft edges, and we did not cut it," he wrote. "Halvah was eaten mostly with black bread, and the best came from the Macedonian who was next door to the pharmacy of Malach who was Maxim Litvinov's uncle. At the Macedonian, we bought bouza [a rice drink] to drink with halvah. It was nonalcoholic, clear and sparkling and sold in a little bottle called a flasche."

He also talked about his arrival in 1929 with four sisters in what was then Palestine, and how he eventually joined the British army, serving for five years in Egypt and Libya. His parents, another sister, and a brother remained in Bialystok.

None survived. His mother and siblings died in a concentration camp. His father was shot in reprisals for the legendary incident involving the resistance hero Yitzhak Malamed, who lived in the Bialystok ghetto and worked in a factory. In February, 1943, when the Jews heard that they were to be exterminated, Malamed and a few others collected bottles of sulphuric acid for defense. On February 5, Nazi police raided a house in the ghetto, and Malamed threw acid into the eyes of one officer, blinding him. The blinded officer fired into the crowd, killing one person, but Yitzhak Malamed fled and hid. When the Jews refused to give him up, the Gestapo rounded up one hundred men, women, and children and marched them to a garden where they were machine-gunned against the wall of the Neivelt prayer house.

Malamed surrendered when he heard that if he did not, the Nazis would kill everyone in the ghetto. He was hanged in the square on the corner of Pietrowska and Malameda Streets, the spot where he had thrown the acid, now commemorated with a black marble plaque. When the rope broke after only a few seconds and his body fell to the ground, it was riddled with bullets. Then the Germans rehung the corpse and left it on display for two days.

As we left, Yerachmiel Giladi gave me the primer *A Practical Course in Esperanto* by Dr. Ferenc Szilágyi, assuring me that it was an easy language to learn. As an example, he said, "Danken pro la kukoj," thanking us for the kuchen.

Too bad I was unable to bid him farewell with "Adiaŭ. ^Gis revido"—Good-bye, until we meet again.

Maybe this year in Jerusalem, I thought the next morning, as we drove along the highway from Tel Aviv to the Holy City with the remaining few kuchen in my handbag. Although stale and dry, they could still be shown as examples if the opportunity arose. I was feeling optimistic because I remembered reading in the classic book *Six Thousand Years of Bread: Its Holy and Unholy History* by H. E. Jacob that a most unusual feature in Jerusalem during the time of Jesus was a special street of professional bread

New York Bagel Bakery, Bialystok, 1998. *Photograph by Boguslaw Florian Skok.*

bakers. "The breads were round," Jacob wrote. "They resembled flat stones slightly raised in the center, and were scarcely thicker than a finger. They were so small that at least three breads were necessary for one man's meal. . . . The Jews' bread was, in point of size, rather like the modern roll." Or, given a depressed center instead of a raised one, rather like a bialy? I could only dream.

After walking around the glowing, antique old city of Jerusalem for just a few hours, Dick and I were struck by the differences between this serious, spiritual place and the lyrical, pleasure-loving Mediterranean Tel Aviv. Even modern buildings in this hilly, piney inland capital must by law be constructed of Jerusalem stone, and that pale, honey-colored quarry stone suggests a cityscape modeled in halvah.

There was much on my agenda for Jerusalem, but nothing took precedence over a visit with Arieh Shamir, the prolific contributor to the *Bialystoker Shtimme*, who had agreed to see me. I asked him to join us for tea or a drink at the American Colony Hotel, where we were staying. Located in East Jerusalem, it is a dream of a Moorish palace with tiled gardens, lemon trees, and fountains and is a traditional hangout for international journalists and writers, including, at one time, Saul Bellow, who is honored in the lobby with a plaque. I was surprised, therefore, that Arieh Shamir refused to meet us at that hotel because, he said, the hotel is in the Arab sector and its owners are said to be sympathetic to the Palestinian cause for a divided Jerusalem. Later, a few other Israelis also refused to meet us there, although many more were regulars at the urbane bar and very good restaurant. And so we met Shamir in the café of the busy and commercial Moriah Jerusalem Hotel.

Immediately familiar-looking with his fair, wispy hair, his pale eyes, and rotund figure, the amiable seventy-four-year-old man reminded me of several uncles in my Ashkenazi family. And we had not talked more than fifteen minutes before he insisted that we have dinner at home with him and his wife, something we could not do but promised for our next visit.

"I arrived in Palestine on November 7, 1938, when I was eighteen," he began. "We were allowed by the British to land at a temporary harbor near Haifa," he said. "It was ten months before war broke out in Europe, and I had a student certificate so I could join my mother and brother who were already here.

"In Bialystok, my father was a printer who used to hand set type. He died in 1927 and left my mother a young and pretty widow. If a man wanted to take her out to a movie or for a walk, she didn't go, because she said people knew her and would talk. Her solution was to leave Bialystok and go to Palestine."

Explaining that he retired as a high-ranking officer of the

Israeli national police force in 1978, Arieh Shamir said he then worked for Hadassah and now writes many articles and book reviews for the *Shtimme* and several other small publications in Israel.

"No one born in Bialystok can forget kuchen. It was the most important and popular food, like a hamburger in your country," he said, adding that he had visited the United States several times, stopping in New York en route to California, where his daughter lives. "Rich Jews ate kuchen with meals, and for poor Jews kuchen were the meal. Sometimes we had kuchen with tea and maybe a piece of smoked herring or other fish, or with a soup of cabbage and potatoes. We bought hot kuchen in stores and from street sellers who carried them in straw baskets, all in the Jewish section, close to the town clock. We ate them in the morning and in the night and in between."

Shamir repeated what he had been told about Jews in Bialystok being overjoyed for a few weeks in 1939, when Molotov and von Ribbentrop, the Russian and German foreign ministers, agreed to the partition of Poland and gave Bialystok to the Russians. "When the Russians came in, the Jews danced in the street, and gave flowers to the soldiers. The Russians used Jews for important work because they did not trust the Polacks. They even had Jews in the KGB. Then on June 21, 1941, Hitler turned on the Soviet Union, took over Bialystok, and the Germans accused the Jews of being Communists. When the soldiers came into the city, they started a pogrom, shouting and shooting and killing Jews and then burning the Great Synagogue. Michael Fliker is getting the Polacks to erect a memorial to the Jews in Bialystok." In August 1995, a monument to the victims of that fire was dedicated in Bialystok.

Shamir saw many fellow Bialystokers at the funeral in Israel of the British publisher and Czech Jew, Robert Maxwell. He would not explain what connection he or the other Bialystokers had with the mysterious Maxwell that drew them to the funeral. Having gone back to Bialystok in 1993 for the fiftieth anniversary of the ghetto's destruction, Shamir returned to Israel disconsolate. "The young Polacks destroyed everything the Nazis did not, even the Jewish cemeteries," he said.

"I eat kuchen in the United States when I visit my daughter in California, but, to tell you the truth, without poppy seeds, they're ridiculous. And I'll tell you something else," Arieh whispered conspiratorially. "Lipa's are not really like those in Bialystok either. First, they are not baked by a wood fire. Then the centers are not crisp enough, because they are pressed with fingers, instead of with a *velgaholze* [a rolling pin—from *velga*, "to roll," and *holze*, "wood"]. But don't tell him I said that."

"Anyway, maybe it's me," Arieh Shamir said a bit downcast. "Now I am old. When you're young, everything is tasty."

NINE

———≫●≪———

BIALYSTOK, ARGENTINA

"Velvl Matinsky, I presume," is what I imagined myself saying were I ever finally to meet this former kuchen baker
from Bialystok who emigrated to Argentina after the Second World War. If my search lacked the drama of Stanley's
journey to find Livingston, its successful conclusion in the
fall of 1999 was no less a victory, one reached by a path that
was typically circuitous for this project.

During the first four years of my research, it seemed that
any meaningful contact with Bialystokers in Argentina
would elude me. I knew from the start that there was a big
community of Polish Jews in Argentina, and I had a few
names from the *Bialystoker Shtimme*, but two telephone
conversations held in smatterings of Spanish, Yiddish, and

English with Wolf Czynski, an Argentine-Jewish furrier I had found through the *Shtimme*, brought just a hint that, yes, there once was a kuchen baker in Buenos Aires, but no, not for many, many years.

I got lucky on May 1, 1996, when an article by Calvin Sims appeared in the *New York Times*, recounting the history of Moisés Ville, a town about a seven-hour drive, 400 miles, north of Buenos Aires, in the Argentine province of Santa Fe. Founded by Russian Jews in 1889 with help from Baron Maurice De Hirsch, a philanthropic French Jew who bought land on which Jews could settle and eventually buy, the town was named for Moses. The settlers became ranchers, gauchos, and farmers who established the country's first agrarian cooperative and introduced crops such as rice and sunflowers. Although the percentage of Jews in the town's population has slipped from 90 to 15 percent (now they number about three hundred), there are still so many vestiges of their customs related to holidays and foods, and so many buildings with Hebrew lettering and stars of David, that many Argentinian Jews make pilgrimages there because, as several are quoted in the *Times* article, this is the one place in the country where they do not feel the pressure of incipient anti-Semitism.

With its 215,000 Jews, Argentina has the largest Jewish population in Latin America, and the sixth-largest in the world, excluding Israel. The decline in the Jewish population of Moisés Ville is due mostly to migration to large cities, especially Buenos Aires, for greater intellectual and professional opportunities. Many Argentinian Jews have also emigrated to Israel.

The most important clue for me in the article was the mention of Anita Weinstein, director of the Mark Turkow Center, a part of AMIA (Associación Mutual Israelita Argentina), which is an umbrella organization of the country's many Jewish cultural and social groups. After wresting the correct telephone number from Buenos Aires information (not easily accomplished because of the many names this organization has and the rapidity with which Buenos Aires telephone numbers are changed), I called Mrs. Weinstein and was delighted to hear that she spoke perfect English. Her first thought was that I was looking for pletzls, of which, she said, there are many, but she drew a blank when I described the bialystoker kuchen and its form.

Among other generous efforts, she put me in touch with Ava Rosenthal, the director of the Moisés Ville town museum, who at first found no traces of the bialys or of any Bialystok descendants, although she eventually discovered one woman who described a sweet, eggy, and atypical example that she called kuchen. As interesting as Moisés Ville might be for its Jewish history, it did not seem worth a visit, given its remoteness and its total lack of hotels and Bialystokers.

A few weeks later, Anita Weinstein wrote: "Good news! I have found a man named Velvl Matinsky, who is 80 and lives in Buenos Aires and who was born in Bialystok, where he baked kuchen. He is willing to tell you anything you want to know, but he speaks only Spanish and Yiddish." Thinking that what the world (and I) needed was a hybrid language—Spiddish or Yanish, or perhaps Esperanto—I almost gave up. I knew it would be virtually impossible to have a worthwhile interview by telephone through an interpreter, and I had no prospects of getting to Argentina.

Three years later, just when this book was as finished as I thought it ever would be, I was given an assignment by *The New Yorker* to write about Argentine beef. I immediately called Anita Weinstein to alert her and to find out, cautiously, if Velvl Matinsky was still alive.

And so, on a bright and sunny day in November 1999, late spring in Argentina, my husband and I left the stylish Recoleta section of Buenos Aires, with its parks and flowering mauve jacaranda trees, its international fashion boutiques, and the posh Alvear Palace, the grande dame of the city's hotels, where we were staying, and took a taxi to Once, the commercial Jewish neighborhood where the AMIA offices are.

Arriving early, we walked around the crowded, vibrant streets of somewhat dilapidated buildings that housed discount stores selling fabrics, furs, bridal gowns, jewelry, electronics, and religious books and objects, just as their counterparts do on New York's Lower East Side and along the rue des Rosiers in Paris. Wanting a light lunch, we went to Succot David, a well-known kosher restaurant serving Argentine parrilla—grilled meat. As Dick and I shared some Israeli-Middle Eastern appetizers (salads of eggplant, peppers, hummus, tabbouleh, falafel and tiny meatballs), we watched families and business groups, the men wearing fedoras or yarmulkes, dig into the mountains of beefsteaks and alpine peaks of fried potatoes. Except for the Spanish interlaced with Yiddish, they could have been sitting around tables at Sammy's Famous Roumanian Restaurant on Chrystie Street in New York.

We approached the new modern AMIA building on Pasteur Street, recognizing it by the blue-and-white Israeli flag. Anita Weinstein had warned us about the tight security at the door and the need to show our passports. Like all other Jewish institutions in Buenos Aires, this one had concrete barricades along the curb and, inside, guards and metal detectors. Such precautions followed the 1994 bombing of AMIA's former headquarters, during which eighty-nine staff members were killed and three hundred were wounded. A list of the victims on a blackboard on the front of the building marks the scene of intermittent protests by Jewish groups, angry that the government has still not found the perpetrators, some of whom are believed to be well-known members of the police force.

Instantly friendly, the petite, dark-haired Anita Weinstein explained that in addition to being prepared to set up an appointment with Velvl Matinsky, she had found another ex-Bialystoker, Abrasha Levy, with whom she had arranged a telephone interview.

We made that call with Anita on the line, in case Levy's English gave out before my Spanish and Yiddish. The most revealing piece of information provided by this ex-Bialystoker was that, indeed, his mother did split the kuchen so they could be used for sandwiches, the only such report I came across.

"It was very common for children to take such sandwiches to school for lunch or snacks," Levy said. "They were delicious filled with an omelet or pastrami or other sliced meat." He also recalled that each day he would leave the family home on Polna Street to buy kuchen on Plisutski Street. Having survived Auschwitz, he left Bialystok in 1946, when he was twenty, and went to Paris, where he obtained papers for Paraguay. But during a stopover in Montevideo, Uruguay, he ran off and sneaked into Argentina. He became a citizen in 1949, when Juan Perón declared an amnesty for all émigrés who had no official papers. For most of his life, he was a tailor specializing in trousers.

"Back in Bialystok, I ate two or three kuchen every day," Levy said. "And even though they were salty, I liked them with sweet things, not halvah, as you ask, but with jam."

We then called Mr. Matinsky and spoke to his wife, who seemed reluctant to meet with us. Anita finally divined that the Matinskys did not want me to go to their home, as I had suggested for their convenience, and as they lived in San Martin, about forty minutes from central Buenos Aires, they wanted a car and driver to take them back and forth. Of course we arranged that for the following day, so we could meet at the Alvear Palace, and I was much relieved when Anita volunteered to serve as interpreter.

The next day at teatime, Anita and I met Velvl Matinsky and his wife, Mina Yabkov. Short, compact and wiry, Velvl had thin, graying hair and about the brightest, most mischievous blue eyes I have ever seen—eyes that followed every pretty waitress in the room. "Velvl Matinsky, I presume," I finally got to say, making a private joke with myself. His plump, rosy-cheeked wife, who was seventy-seven, seemed nervous as she kept glancing uneasily around the chic, glassed-in Orangerie tearoom. Both carried gifts for me—a box of chocolate bonbons and a bagful of frozen small pletzls that turned out to smell and taste like first cousins of bialys in New York.

Velvl Matinsky explained how he hid out as a partisan in the woods around Bialystok for three and a half years. "Everyone told me I would never make it—that if the Germans or the Poles didn't kill me, I would starve to death. But I stole food and ate what I could find in the forest, and here I am at eighty-three, and have my first great-grandchild," he said, adding that some of his children and grandchildren live in Israel, where he and his wife visit each year.

Before the Germans arrived in Bialystok, he baked kuchen in his family's bakery, getting up at three in the morning so that the first batch would come out of the oven around five or five thirty, when customers began to line up to buy kuchen for 7 groschen. He recalled that women who sold kuchen in baskets in the street, bought them for 5.50 groschen and also sold them for 7. "We made them with flour, water, salt, and yeast—*nada más*," he said, confirming the use of the little rolling-pin I sketched for him.

After the German defeat, Velvl emerged from the woods and Mina, also a native of Bialystok, found her way back. Velvl was in the town square with some friends, all wondering what to do next, when Mina approached. One of the friends knew her, but Velvl did not, even though, as they soon discovered, they were distant cousins. Before long, they decided to live together and marry, and after a year they had their first son. In 1947, Velvl wanted to leave, as none of their immediate family had survived and he was depressed by Bialystok. Mina's aunt, already in Argentina, sent them tickets, and they traveled through France to Le Havre. Once in Argentina, they joined other Bialystokers in a settlement known as Villa Lynch.

"Most were in textiles," Velvl recalled, "and they introduced a lot of modern machinery to Argentina." Known in its heyday as a "Jewish Manchester" because of the preponderance of mills and textile workers, Villa Lynch had a thriving Bialystok community, with synagogues, libraries, Yiddish theater, and schools. Anita Weinstein explained that Villa Lynch still has a small Jewish community and a few textile mills, but that competition from inexpensive foreign imports has greatly diminished their number.

"After I was in Argentina for a while," Velvl Matinsky continued, "I started to make kuchen for a baker who offered me a partnership, but Mina said no, because bakers always lived over their stores and she didn't want to. So I continued to work for her relatives in their textile mill. But to tell you the truth, I always would rather have made kuchen."

Showing the numbers tattooed on her forearm in one of many concentration camps (including one where she narrowly escaped some of Dr. Mengele's infamous experiments), Mina explained that she has many *recuerdos malos*—bad memories—of her time under the Nazis.

"There is hardly a night when one of us doesn't wake up screaming," Mina said. "It always used to frighten our children when they were small."

The day before we were to leave Buenos Aires, Anita Weinstein called on a final note of triumph. She had managed to find Armando Bublik, the author of the novel *Poncho y Talmud*. It is a story of several generations of a family between 1920 and 1950 in Bialystok, Argentina, where Bublik's great-grandparents settled in 1895 after leaving Bialystok, Poland, and where he himself was born and raised.

"Bialystok, Argentina?" I asked, not quite believing what I had heard. It was the first time anyone had told me that there actually was a place in Argentina called Bialystok. I was devastated to hear it, since we were leaving Argentina the following morning. Armando Bublik said that it was a sort of suburb of Moisés Ville and, in keeping with the practice at the turn of the century, was named for the settlers' native city. He said that he never saw Bialystok, Argentina, on any map other than one in the museum in Moisés Ville, and that it now has only about thirty houses and a small synagogue. He also said that for the past fifty years, present and former Jewish inhabitants of Moisés Ville and Bialystok and their descendants hold a reunion dinner on the last Friday in November; in 1999, about a hundred and twenty attended.

An ophthalmologist by day, Dr. Bublik writes at night, staying slim and fit by going to a gym, as he and his wife were going to do after a Sunday brunch with us. They, too, brought a gift, this time deliciously crisp, cinnamon- and nut-flavored cookies called kamischbrot.

"My great-grandfather owned a textile mill in Poland, but after a bloody pogrom he said, 'This land Poland is sick. I don't want to live here.' He gave the factory to his workers and took his family to Brussels, where he said that they would take the first ship going to America—South or North. He was not lucky. The first ship went to South America, so here I am."

Like almost every Jew I spoke to in Argentina, Armando Bublik always wished that his family had emigrated to the United States. Although official, overt anti-Semitism has long since disappeared in Argentina, every Jew I spoke to save one felt that it exists in this Catholic country, in certain professions and among the military. They cite the failure of the government to hunt down those who bombed AMIA headquarters and the more severe treatment meted out to Jews who were among the 33,000 Argentinians who disappeared (most never to be found or heard of again) in the "Dirty War" between 1976 and 1983. The one exception, a very wealthy, elderly Jewish financier and rancher who has managed to remain in favor with various Argentinian regimes (and whose name I withhold so as not to embarrass the friends who introduced us), assured me that there was no more anti-Semitism in Argentina than in the United States and that Jews generally brought their troubles on themselves because they were inclined to be "leftists."

Although Buenos Aires was the last stop on my worldwide bialy tour, I consider it unfinished business. I am determined, just for my own curiosity, to visit Moisés Ville, Villa Lynch, and of course, Bialystok, Argentina, and I expect some day to do so.

BIALYSTOKERS DOWN UNDER

Although I succeeded in getting the assignments that would take me to every Bialystoker outpost I knew of in Paris, Israel, Buenos Aires, and around the United States, I was not able to wangle a trip to Melbourne, Australia. It is something I much regret, because during the last five years of my research, I corresponded with and spoke to several of the friendliest, most gracious and forthcoming Bialystoker émigrés anywhere.

I was surprised, in fact, to learn that Australia was such fertile soil for my search, with some forty-five thousand Polish Jews living in and around Melbourne, while Sydney had attracted Jews from Hungary and Germany.

· · ·

My first clue about Bialystokers "down under" came from a moving, detailed memoir in a 1994 issue of the Bialystoker Shtimme, written by Paul "Pesach" Szmusz of Camberwell, a prosperous suburb of Melbourne. Izaak Rybal at the Bialystok Center obliged with an address, and my letter about my search for memories of bialys on their native ground, and, possibly, versions in Australia, brought forth one of the real treasures of this project.

Explaining that he was born in Bialystok in 1921 and went to Australia in 1948 because he had a cousin there who was his only surviving relative, Mr. Szmusz wrote, "If I had some money, I would have run right back to Poland." When I later telephoned him just to hear his voice, I asked why he had not come to New York. "That is the question I ask myself every single day," answered this gentle, polite, and humorous man, who passed away in 1997. He assured me that no Bialystok kuchen baker would have emigrated to Australia, because "it was always considered the end of the world." A retired accountant, Mr. Szmusz was also a Yiddishist, with a master's degree in the language and its literature.

He assured me that he had a fantastic memory, and certainly his recollections of the kuchen and the city of their origin more than prove his point.

I am answering your questions about Bialystoker kuchen with great pleasure. This kuchen was specific to Bialystok. Nowhere else in Poland or old Russia did the Jewish bakers make that kuchen and other Jewish people in Poland made fun of us, and called us "Bialystoker kuchen fressers." But when some of them visited our town, the first thing they did was to taste our kuchen and buy dozens to take back home.

The kuchen goes back many years. When I was about 7, my great-grandmother told me that when she was my age in the 1850s, she would come down in the afternoon to her father's bakery and watch her mother and her 12-year-old sister roll out the kuchen dough and she would help by putting on the onions and the poppy seeds.

Bialystok was a Jewish town with Jews rich and poor—more poor than rich. My father was a tailor and we were four kids. Life was not so easy. Meat was only eaten on the Sabbath if my mother's finances could afford it. Many weekdays a plate of soup and a kuchen were our meal. We were used to eating kuchen from childhood and loved them.

In the 1920s and 1930s, every little street in our

Bialystok had its own small kuchen bakery. The owner was the baker with his sons, sons-in-law, wife and daughters working with him. Everything was done by hand. The men would finish baking about five or six in the morning, then go to sleep and let the women do the selling. About midday, the father-baker would come down and start mixing the kuchen dough from flour, water, yeast and salt and leave it to rise. Then the women would take over, rolling the dough into two sizes—a small one that sold for 5 groschen and a larger size for 10 groschen. The women rolled the dough with two rolling pins. One woman used a regular rolling pin to shape a round about six-inches across and one-inch thick. Then the other woman would take over with her special rolling pin that had a two-inch center [the accompanying drawing shows a cylinder] that pressed down the center.

She would brush the top of each kuchen with water, put on finely cut onion rings and poppy-seeds and place four to six kuchen on a big wooden spade [a peel] and pass it to the baker at the oven. He would lay them flat on the right side of the oven floor against the flames of the fire that was always made with dry pine-wood. It let out a nice aroma that gave the crust a very special taste. The kuchen would bake in ten minutes and cus-

tomers would already be waiting to grab them as soon as they came out of the oven. They were brown and crisp on top and the center was like a crisp matzoh but maybe a little thicker. Very tasty indeed.

The most popular kuchen baker was Moishe Mendl. He had his bakery right in town with entrances from both Kupiecka and Gieldowa streets. People would come from all over the city for his kuchen and he was very proud of them. He made only the larger size with plenty of onion and poppy-seeds.

Not all bakeries made kuchen in the afternoon, some did so only in the morning. Many bakeries were on streets where the Jewish working class lived. The rich people ate kuchen sometimes, but the poor would eat them everyday. There was Moishe-Griske the kuchen baker of Mazoiecka Street, and Piaskes Long-Nose on Zelazna Street, and Sholem-Maike on Sosnova Street opposite the old Jewish cemetery. Berl-Amolek was on the Shul-hof and Yosl-the-Deaf-One was on the Fish-markt. They are only a few of the many.

Some people would buy kuchen from the bakeries and sell them from baskets near the Shul-hof and we young boys and girls would go there late in the evening after school and buy a few to eat on the way home. Many evenings, we were too late and none were left.

I asked Mr. Szmusz if he recalled eating kuchen with halvah. "Yes, we did eat kuchen with halvah from a shop called the Macedonian," he answered. "There were two such shops that were like coffeehouses, where you could buy halvah to take with you or sit at a table and eat it with a drink made of rice that was called bouza, sold in very small bottles. It was made on the premises, like the halvah. One such place was on Rynek Kosciuszko opposite the Town Clock, and the other was on Senkiewicza Street. Generally we ate kuchen with butter or cheese, always spreading them on top, over the onions. It was also very tasty with kosher sausage. Kuchen were good with everything."

Reporting on bialys he had tasted on a visit to New York, Mr. Szmusz wrote, "All I can say is that for us, the older generation, the New York kuchen did not have the taste of the originals. They are all right for the Jewish people born in America. They don't know the difference. The nearest in taste to the originals are those I have eaten from an Arabic baker in Jerusalem, baked in front of the flame of a wood fire. They did not have the kuchen shape and no onions or poppy-seeds, but were very tasty."

Pesach Szmusz's detailed reminiscence of the bialy was perhaps the most complete I garnered, but not the only one from Australia. About a year after I returned from Israel, and having stayed in touch with Arieh Shamir, the retired police officer and writer who lives in Jerusalem, I received a letter from him saying that he had just reviewed a new book, *Jewels and Ashes*, written by an Australian, Arnold Zable. He thought it might help in my research, as it was a Bialystok memoir.

A writer of childrens' books, articles, and short stories, Mr. Zable was born in New Zealand to parents who emigrated from Bialystok, where their original family name had been Zabludowski, one of the oldest and most prominent in that region. Hearing about his parents' home all of his life, Arnold Zable visited Bialystok in 1990 and described that experience, along with a beautifully written account of the entwined histories of the city and his family: "Bialystok was their siren's song, a spell that had bewitched generation after generation, an enticing melody which forever hinted at deliverance; and even when all that remained was a wasteland of rubble, survivors had still returned with the faint hope that they would rediscover their ancient vision, their lost dream."

What was unsettling to me was that there wasn't a single mention of kuchen in all of that lovely text. There was just one reference to bread when a Polish-Jewish immigrant, newly arrived in Melbourne, told Arnold Zable's father that he hid from the Nazis in Bialystok and was regularly given a loaf of fresh bread from the bakery of Etel Zabludowski, a cousin of the Zables. "He retained an image of it in the ensuing years," Zable wrote, "for there came a time when even the memory of a slice of bread was like manna from heaven."

"So was that bread by any chance a kuchen?" I asked Arnold Zable when I telephoned him.

"I don't know, but I doubt it," he answered. "The only place I ever heard of the kuchen, or what you call bialys, was when I was in New York in 1970, 1973, and 1993. I do not remember my parents ever speaking of them," he said. Zable explained that his father was not food-oriented, but his mother was a good cook. Zable himself had been educated in a Yiddish-speaking school in Melbourne.

Fortunately, he referred me to Felix Flicker, a friend in Melbourne who left Bialystok in 1940 at the age of fifteen, and to his wife, Ursula. "She works for the Holocaust Center in Australia," Zable said, "and is obsessed with Bialystok and knows everything about it, as does her husband." He kindly gave me the Flickers' telephone number and promised to call them and explain my project.

"Remember bialystoker kuchen?" Felix Flicker said to my immediate relief when I called him. "And how I remember! I can still taste it on my tongue. Every part of the city and the suburbs had kuchen bakeries. I ate the kuchen with butter or cheese and did not split it but cut the round into quarters, which wasn't easy because it was puffy on the rim but crisp in the center.

"I personally do not believe in eating halvah with kuchen or any other bread. Halvah is a meal in itself. But some people did eat the kuchen with halvah. Some people ate halvah with you name it. . . .

"Say, Mimi, has anyone mentioned to you a kuchen baker named Moishe Mendl?"

When I told him that Pesach Szmusz had, Felix Flicker said, "I'm so glad you're in touch with him. He is twelve to fifteen years older than I am, and he remembers more. But considering that I was only fifteen when I left, I remember a lot. In those days a bar mitzvah boy was already a mensch [a mature, responsible person]. Today a bar mitzvah boy is still a child.

"Kuchen were always warm from the oven. Each bakery made ten or twelve lots a day. Any time of the day was right for them—breakfast, lunch, and dinner, even with meat. We did not believe in eating meat without bread.

"We were lucky. My whole family—mother, father, brother, sister and I—all came to Australia and so avoided the Holocaust."

I began to feel I had come full circle when Felix Flicker said, "The kuchen most like those I remember from Bialystok are in Gedera, Israel, where my friend Lipa Avinadov taught a Yemenite baker to make them. It is a known fact that at large gatherings, Lipa will bring a sackful of them. New York bialys were very close to Bialystok's when I had them about thirty-five years ago, but I can't say about now."

Unlike Pesach Szmusz, Felix Flicker recalled one Avrom Ostrobuski, a baker who arrived in Melbourne in 1947 or 1948 and who baked kuchen for special occasions, but not for his regular retail trade.

What I began to think of as my own Bialy Interpol took shape as I introduced my Austin contact, Roy Mersky, to the Flickers, when Mersky was guest lecturer at a seminar in Melbourne. He reported sharing a most hospitable Friday-night dinner at their home, where he met the Flickers' son-in-law, Paul Forgasz, who planned to visit New York a few months later. I called Felix Flicker to be sure that he would give Paul our telephone number, and he, Dick, and I had a pleasant dinner together. The headmaster of the Mount Scopus Memorial College, a Jewish school, Paul Forgasz seemed like an instant old friend and another valued addition to my strange but rapidly growing bialy network. Although we have never met, whenever I have called the Flickers to verify facts, Ursula greets me with a warmly intimate, "Hello, Mimi! How is your husband?" I still hope to get to Melbourne to meet these friends with whom I share the camaraderie common to Bialystoker kuchen fressers the world over.

The story of Bialystok and its kuchen was summed up most eloquently in the letter from Pesach Szmusz.

In June, 1941 the Nazis came to us and since then there are no more bialystoker kuchen and no more kuchen bakeries and no more of our Bialystok Jews. The Nazis killed almost all of us. I was in Auschwitz and other concentration camps with Samuel Pisar, and I was liberated in Dachau, then spent four months in a tuberculosis hospital. I went back to Bialystok and left shortly with a curse on my lips and a promise never to return to that cursed land and people again.

Poland was the only country where young Jews were killed after the war. I don't forgive the Nazis, but I don't forgive the Poles either. When the Nazis came to Bialystok on June 27th, 1941, Poles showed them where the Jews lived and Poles robbed the Jewish houses. The Nazis did not build Auschwitz, Treblinka or Maidanek in France, Belgium or Holland. They built them in Poland because they knew the Poles would help them kill the Jews. The Poles were partners in our destruction.

Please forgive me for expressing my thoughts. I was 20 years old in the Bialystok ghetto, 23 years old in Auschwitz, and 100 years older after the liberation. I am still not liberated and I will not be free until my last day.

And this is the story of the bialystoker kuchen. I do not think that any Bialystoker can tell you more.

MIMI SHERATON

Photograph by Yasushi Egami.

———=»•«=———

THE MAKING OF A BIALY

In the true spirit of bialy culture, and for the full experience of entering the fragrant domain of the bialy bakery with its bustle and air of savory expectancy, bialys should be store-bought. But because I have not found any really good bialys other than Kossar's in the United States, and because many may be reluctant to order by telephone (212-473-4810), via the website (www.kossarsbialys.com), or through e-mail (mail@kossarsbialys.com), I offer the following recipe as the best second choice.

It has been devised with the help of the bakers at Kossar's bakers, who warned me, correctly, that I would not get results that exactly matched theirs. Not only is there a big

———=»•«=———

difference in the ovens (theirs is a brick-lined convection oven with revolving iron shelves, while home ovens are metal-lined with rack shelves), but also because the dough develops differently in large batches, the Kossar recipe consisting of 100 pounds of flour, 7 gallons of water, 2 pounds of salt, and 1 pound of yeast for a yield of 70 to 80 dozen, which is a little more than you might need. Whitey Aquanno said that he has tried to make small batches, but they didn't come out quite the same, for reasons even he doesn't understand.

Using the right ingredients allows for a fighting chance at authenticity, and anyone determined to try this should use only high-gluten, unbleached bread flour (wheat, but not whole wheat) that has no dough conditioner, fresh, moist bakers' cake yeast, and kosher coarse salt that is not iodized or coarse sea salt. (Bread flour, bakers' yeast, and the salt are available at some supermarkets and at most health-food stores.) Bottled still water should be used in areas where tap water has an off flavor. Ordinary flour, salt, and powdered yeast will work, of course, but at a great sacrifice of flavor and texture. Given all of the time and effort involved, it seems pointless to use any but the most correct ingredients. One advantage to making your own bialys is that you can add poppy seeds, but taste those carefully before using them (and if possible before buying them), to be sure that they are not rancid. To keep them fresh, store them in the refrigerator.

Because bakers' yeast purchased in a supermarket is often stale (despite its expiration date) and, therefore, inactive, and because the usual method of pretesting yeast in water with a little sugar does not apply here, test as follows. Buy 2 ounces yeast and cut in half. Mash half into $1/2$ cup of warm water and stir in $1/2$ teaspoon of sugar. Cover loosely and set aside in a warm corner to see if it froths up within 10 minutes. If so, assume that the remaining yeast will also be active. Discard the test yeast.

Home ovens can be improved for bialy baking in several ways. If the oven has a convection option, it should be used for this. Also, to get a good crust on the bottom of the bialys, bake them directly on a preheated pizza stone placed on the shelves of the oven. Otherwise, use a large, metal preheated cookie sheet or jelly-roll pan on each shelf. A pizza oven would certainly be good for baking bialys.

To make 12 to 14 bialys, each $3^1/2$ to 4 inches in diameter, you will need about $1^1/2$ to 2 pounds or about 5 to 6 cups of high-gluten bread flour, about 3 cups very cold water (tap or bottled), 2 tablespoons noniodized kosher coarse salt or coarse sea salt, and $1/2$ ounce of fresh bakers' yeast. For the topping, use 1 medium-size sweet white onion (a scant cupful when finely chopped) and about 2 tablespoons of coarse, toasted bread crumbs. (Kossar's uses crumbs made of dried, ground bialys, but if you had bialys to begin with, you would not need to bake them.) If using poppy seeds, you will need about 3 tablespoons or a little more than $1/2$ ounce.

The onion topping is best prepared 3 to 5 hours before it will be used, so that it will soften slightly, and the harshest aroma and flavor of the onions will evaporate. Peel and chop onion very fine. For best results, do this with a chopping knife or, as second choice, through the fine blade of a meat grinder. (With such a small amount of onion, it's hardly worth cleaning the parts of a grinder for this operation.) Do not use a food processor or blender, as the onion will become too liquid.

Thoroughly mix 1 tablespoon of crumbs into the chopped onions and set the mixture aside, loosely covered; reserve the extra crumbs. After about 3 hours, check to see if the mixture has thickened to the texture of loose wet sand. If it is too liquid, add more crumbs a half-teaspoonful at a time, waiting 10 minutes between each addition.

To prepare the dough, mash yeast into $1/2$ cup cold water. When dissolved, stir into the remaining cold water. Turn 5 cups of flour and the salt into the bowl of an electric mixer and, using the dough hook, beat in the yeast water. Slowly beat flour and water, adding more flour gradually only if the mixture is too sticky, or a little more water if it is too stiff, but err on the side of stickiness. Raise the mixer speed to medium and beat only until the mixture holds together but is still sticky. Gather the dough and place it in a clean, large, unoiled glass or ceramic bowl. Cover the bowl loosely with a towel and set it in a warm, draft-free corner. Let it rise for three to three-and-a-half hours, or until double in volume, or until an indentation made with a finger springs back into place. (Time will vary with the warmth in the room. If it is a very cold day, place the loosely covered bowl in an oven that is turned off but that has a pilot light.)

At this point, you can try to knead the dough with the dough hook of the mixer for about 10 minutes. However, because the dough is thick and sticky, some older models of home mixers should be run only at the first or second speeds to avoid burning out the motor. After 10 minutes, or instead of using the dough hook, turn the risen dough out on a lightly floured board. Knead by hand for 5 to 10 minutes, if you have used the dough hook, or 15 to 20 minutes, if you have not. A dough scraper is essential for this. The dough should be smooth, elastic and blistered. Work in additional flour only if needed.

Shape it into a ball and place it back in the mixing bowl and cover loosely with a towel. Let it rise in a warm, draft-free corner for about $1^1/_2$ hours, or until a depression made with a finger springs back into place.

Punch down the risen dough. Divide into four portions and roll each of these between the palms of your hands into ropes that are about 2 inches in diameter. From each rope, cut or pinch off three or four pieces. Roll each gently but firmly into a ball between lightly floured hands. Cover the shaped rolls to prevent them from drying out as you work the remainder. When all rolls are formed, cover them with a kit and let them rest for 45 minutes.

Slide pizza stone or baking sheets onto shelves in the lower third of the oven and preheat to 450 degrees.

To form the center indentations on the rolls, work with well-floured hands and lift each round of dough slightly off the work surface and slip the index and middle fingers of both hands underneath, with both thumbs working on top. Press and lightly stretch the center bottom dough, forming a well (but not a hole) and leaving about a $1^1/_2$-inch rim of unpressed dough. Or, using a small glass or jar with a completely flat bottom that is $1^1/_2$ to 2 inches in diameter, press down very firmly in the center of each flattened round and twist to spread dough, then spread lightly with your fingers. Using the sides of your hands, reshape the rims of each bialy. Keep the bialys covered until all are shaped.

When all bialys are formed, add the onion topping. If you

are going to use poppy seeds, brush the tops of bialys with water so that the seeds will stick; that is not necessary if you are using onions only. Dip your slightly cupped index, middle, and fourth fingers into the onion-crumb mixture and smear about a scant teaspoonful over each bialy, being sure to get a thin coating in the well and around its top edge and spreading the well slightly again. Then sprinkle about $1/2$ teaspoonful of poppy seeds over each bialy.

Using a flat, wide spatula as a peel, place the bialys on the preheated baking surface, leaving about a 1-inch space between each on all sides

Bake 15 to 20 minutes, or until the bialys are as golden brown as you want them to be, my choice being for a deep brown (but not black) color. Remove from the baking surface, and you're on your own. Eat (or sell) them as soon as you can. If you plan to freeze any bialys, let them cool on a rack for 10 minutes before wrapping.

NOTE: If you use baking sheets or a pizza tile, you will be able to change the position of the bialys easily during baking. Start them in the lower third of the oven and, after 10 minutes, slide the sheets onto a shelf in the upper third of the oven. That way the onions are less likely to burn and bottoms become crisp.

Several strengths of high-gluten bread flour are available by mail from King Arthur Flour in Norwich, Vermont. For

The Baker's Catalogue, call 1-800-827-6836 or order at www.KingArthurFlour.com.

The strongest Sir Lancelot High-Gluten Flour is best left to experienced bread bakers. The easier but still excellent choice is the Unbleached All-Purpose Bread Flour, and for those used to preparing bread in machines, try the Special for Machines Bread Flour. All are high-gluten.

BIBLIOGRAPHY

The following books and film provided me with invaluable insights into the Jewish life and history of Bialystok and other areas in Poland.

BOOKS

Bialystoker Memorial Book, The. New York: Empire Press, Brooklyn, and the Bialystok Center, 228 East Broadway, New York, NY 10002. 1982.

Dobroszycki, Lucjan, and Barbara Kirshenblatt-Gimblett. *Image Before My Eyes: A Photographic History of Jewish Life in Poland, 1864–1939.* New York: Schocken Books and the YIVO Institute for Jewish Research. 1977.

Kaufman, Jonathan. *A Hole in the Heart of the World: Being Jewish in Eastern Europe.* New York: Viking. 1997.

Melamed, Leo, with Bob Tamarkin. *Escape to the Futures.* New York: John Wiley & Sons. 1996.

Pisar, Samuel. *Of Blood and Hope.* New York: Macmillan. 1979.

Ratner, Max and Betty, with Shirley Blum Tanzer, editor and interviewer. *The Ratner House: A Visual and Oral Hisory, 1888–1988, from Bialystok, Russia/Poland, to Cleveland, Ohio, U.S.A.* 1988.

Sohn, David, compiler and editor. *Bialystok: Photo Album of a Renowned City and Its Jews the World Over.* New York: Bialystoker Alumni Committee. 1951.

Wisniewski, Tomasz. *Jewish Bialystok and Surroundings in Eastern Poland: A Travel Guidebook.* Foreword by Mimi Sheraton. Ipswich, MA: Ipswich Press. 1998.

Tomasz Wisniewski can be contacted for genealogical research or historical data on the Jews of Bialystok and surrounding regions and for photographic archives. E-mail: tomekwisniewski@vena.telbank.pl

Zable, Arnold. *Jewels and Ashes*. New York: Harcourt Brace & Co. 1991.

Zabuski, Charles "Shleimeh," as told to June Sutz Brott. *Needle and Thread: A Tale of Survival from Bialystok to Paris*. P.O. Box 2458, Berkeley, CA 94702: Popincourt Press. 1996.

FILM

Jewish Life in Bialystok, 1939 (videocassette). This fifteen-minute film is distributed by the National Center for Jewish Film, Brandeis University, Lown Building, Room 102, Waltham, MA 12254-9110.